Unexpected Gifts

PALMETTO
PUBLISHING
Charleston, SC
www.PalmettoPublishing.com

Copyright © 2024 by Sara Hathor

All rights reserved

No portion of this book may be reproduced, stored in a retrieval system, or transmitted in any form by any means–electronic, mechanical, photocopy, recording, or other–except for brief quotations in printed
reviews, without prior permission of the author.

Hardcover ISBN: 9798822961319
Paperback ISBN: 9798822961128
eBook ISBN: 9798822961135

Unexpected Gifts

From all the wrong men

SARA HATHOR

Contents

Introduction 1
Prologue 3
The Starter Marriage 6
Love 18
Life after Love 35
Third Time's a Charm? 51
The Revolving Door 82
Conclusion 114
Epilogue 125
References 131
About the Author 133

Introduction

What I'm about to share is a bit revealing, maybe even a tad embarrassing. I'm laying out my fears and flaws, hoping it's not just enlightening but also entertaining, with a dash of hopefulness sprinkled throughout. Every word in this book is true, told from my perspective. To respect everyone's privacy, I've changed all the names—except for the dogs. Their names stay because they embody pure goodness and are already perfect as they are. Honestly, we humans are too, imperfections included.

I express genuine gratitude and appreciation for all the men and loved ones who play a part in this story. It hasn't always been easy, but the growth and love that came out of it all have made every twist and turn worthwhile.

The chapters in this book follow the chronological events of my life. If you're seeking insights on toxic relationships, especially narcissism, how to break free, and understanding attachment styles, start with chapter 1, "The Starter Marriage." For a glimpse into how a seemingly perfect relationship unraveled, along with a bit of Gottman's relationship research, turn to chapter 2, "Love."

For guidance on coping with grief, chapter 3, "Life after Love" is for you. If you're ready to tackle stubborn patterns, understand their roots, and set healthier boundaries, check out chapter 4, "Third Time's a Charm?" Curious about the world of modern dating? Chapter 5, "The Revolving Door" offers a revealing look.

To explore the benefits of solitude, what happens when dreams don't materialize, and the power of prayer, dive into chapter 6, "Conclusion." And if you want to know how the story wraps up, don't miss the epilogue. Finally, for those interested in further reading on any of these topics, the references section has you covered.

Enjoy the journey!

Prologue

As I sat in my therapist Evelyn's office, I revisited a familiar encounter with my ex-husband—one that, even after all these years, continued to affect my self-esteem and relationships with other men.

"When I told Jason I needed more time, he completely lost it. He started screaming, 'Sign the fucking papers, you stupid bitch!' His voice was seething with anger as he ranted about how he'd given me everything—a home, a good life. I owed him this. It was scary and manipulative."

"And then what did you do?" asked Evelyn.

"I tried to walk away, but he warned me not to. So, I stopped. I looked at him and argued again that we didn't make $350,000 that year. We made $56,000 combined, since we were both graduate students at the time. I didn't want to sign the papers because I wasn't sure if it was legal. That's when he flew into another one of his rages."

"What happened? What do you remember?"

"I remember his fists clenching, his eyes darkening, and his face contorting with rage. He stared at me, and it felt like his presence filled the room. He was like a wild animal on the brink of attacking. I thought he might punch the wall or hurl the TV across the room. To defuse the tension, I sat down on the couch and let him vent. It felt safer that way.

"He yelled for what felt like an eternity. I tuned him out and didn't dare argue back. When he finally quieted down, I went to the bedroom to snuggle with the dogs. It became routine. It would take me days to recover. Looking back, that's when my migraines started too."

"That's not surprising. Did you end up signing the papers?"

"Yes," I replied quietly, my gaze falling in shame.

Evelyn spoke gently. "You were married to a narcissist and a bully. It was abusive, even though he never laid a hand on you. Though I believe, if you had stayed, it might have escalated to that. I've worked with many intelligent, accomplished women like you who find themselves in abusive relationships. Some never find the strength to leave. You did."

"Sometimes he could be really nice."

"That's part of the cycle. The cycle of abuse starts with tension, then an outburst like what you described. After that comes the 'hearts and flowers' phase where apologies and kindness follow, and then calm until the tension builds again."

"He never really apologized afterward."

"The 'hearts and flowers' phase can also involve minimizing or ignoring the incident. Now we need to focus on establishing your boundaries. Weak boundaries led you into this situation and are why you're struggling now. It's like the movie *The Runaway*

Bride—she always ordered her eggs to match her partner's preference without knowing her own. That's you."

"I do know how I like my eggs. Scrambled."

"What if someone served you over-easy eggs? Would you politely decline or eat them to avoid offense?"

"I'd probably try them to be polite."

"So, you know your preferences but sometimes prioritize others' feelings over your own to be liked?"

"Maybe sometimes…"

With a compassionate smile, Evelyn said, "We have our work cut out for us."

The Starter Marriage

Until you make the unconscious conscious, it will direct your life and you will call it fate.

—CG Jung

The day after Christmas, I found myself in the basement, staring at six years' worth of stuff, trying to sort out what belonged to me and what belonged to him. It was a stark contrast to the magic of seven Christmases ago when Jason proposed. He'd wrapped the engagement ring in a series of boxes, each one bigger than the last, like those Russian nesting dolls. He couldn't wait until Christmas to give it to me, and I knew him well enough to guess what was inside those boxes. Suddenly, I was engaged, and planning to move to a small Midwestern town where Jason was studying for his PhD in biology.

We'd met in college five years earlier, both of us twenty years old. Jason was a TA in my anatomy class and offered to help me study. With his round face, short dark-blond hair, hazel eyes, and even smile, he was cute in his glasses, radiating a nerdy charm. On our first study date, he showed up late at the library, sat across from me, extended his hand, and said, "Look how steady my hand is; that's the hand of a future surgeon." Despite his overconfidence, he was charming. He patiently explained cellular functions, then suggested we grab dessert. What stood out was how he genuinely wanted to know about my life, unlike most college guys. He walked me to my door that night and gave me a sweet, hopeful kiss.

As we dated, I was touched by his sensitivity. He was always there for me—cheering me on during tough school times, supporting me through friend arguments, and nursing me back to health when I was sick. But Jason had always struggled socially and often felt isolated. Back then, I had the upper hand socially, but I understood his shyness and saw the real Jason. I think being with me gave him a sense of belonging he craved.

Jason felt like my best friend, and we married at twenty-five. That's when things started changing. Jason became the star—a respected grad student with family wealth—while I settled for a secretarial job in our small Midwestern town. He liked reminding me how much smarter he was, how he had the money, and how without him, I wouldn't have a life. When I disagreed, he'd explode. His face twisted, his voice got sharp, his posture grew threatening, and if we were in the car, he drove like a maniac. It was terrifying.

But there were moments when he was the sweet Jason I fell for in college, which made everything confusing. We tried couples counseling, but it focused more on Jason's supposed depression than our marriage. His depression, and his meanness, never seemed to get better. Over time, my self-esteem sank, which only made things worse. He didn't respect me, and I stopped liking or respecting him. But we were married.

One winter evening, five years into our marriage, after yet another emotional beating, I realized Jason wouldn't change. Something inside me shifted, and I mentally checked out of the marriage. Then one October night, an overwhelming feeling hit me: if I ever wanted to do something about my marriage, it had to be that night. I'm not usually one to pick up on cosmic hints, but that night felt different—like the Universe was shouting at me. Without that push, I don't think I would've found the courage. So I blurted out, "I'm not happy." Determined to make Jason take me seriously, I packed up and went to stay with my mom. He cried and pleaded with me not to leave, but by 10 p.m. that Sunday, I was at my mom's door, and my life changed forever.

At first, there were tears and a deep sadness—I can't quite remember why I felt that way, but at the time, I was devastated. Actually, devastated might not be the right word. I think shocked is closer to how I felt. Having Jason in my life was familiar, even though it was unbalanced and dysfunctional. Then came the guilt and the nagging question: "What have I done—walking out on my marriage? I was content enough."

After some serious reflection, though, I reached the conclusion that Jason was a total jerk and it was mostly his fault, and I was certain I'd find the perfect guy in no time because, let's face it, I've got this!

This new chapter in my life took me on a journey I believed would lead to finding true love. Instead, I found myself stuck in recurring patterns, enduring one heartbreak after another, and mastering the skill of letting go and starting anew repeatedly. I share this to offer comfort, a bit of humor, and the reassurance that none of us are navigating life's ups and downs alone.

Plus, maybe I can sprinkle in a nugget of wisdom or two from all the lessons I've picked up along the way!

One of the earliest lessons I learned was about Jason's narcissistic traits. Narcissists usually see themselves as better than others and tend to lack empathy, compassion, or genuine concern for anyone else unless it benefits them. They often have an inflated sense of self-importance and entitlement, always looking for attention and admiration. Whether it's through blatant arrogance or subtle charm, they manipulate others to get what they want. These traits are common in today's society, where narcissism can range from mild self-centeredness to severe emotional and, sometimes, even physical abuse. This spectrum makes it tough for those in relationships with narcissists to fully recognize the harm being done. It's like the frog being dropped into slowly boiling water—not realizing the danger until it's too late—unlike the immediate reaction if the frog were dropped into boiling water all at once.

In my marriage, Jason's narcissism showed up in comments like "You won't have a life without me" or "No one could love you like I do," along with cruel remarks about my intelligence and worth as a partner. He'd conveniently blame his anger on me, treating me like I didn't deserve love or respect—in fact, he once told me he saw me as nothing more than a piece of furniture. He tightly controlled our finances and decisions, shutting down any input from me. His sense of entitlement wasn't just limited to our home; it showed in how he treated store clerks and ignored my mom's feelings to the point where she stopped calling me at home.

During our divorce, Jason proudly claimed his counselor said he was mentally healthy, and dismissed the idea of more sessions. But his behavior told a different story, like the changed locks, the emptied bank account, and the finding of a used condom in our home when I returned—my belongings and our dogs still inside.

Living with a narcissist feels like riding on an emotional rollercoaster. You're constantly on edge, afraid of setting them off. Their unpredictable behavior leaves you confused, often blaming yourself for things you didn't even cause. At home, the tension builds up, making you feel powerless, ignored, and unable to stand up for yourself. Arguments go nowhere, leaving you drained and questioning who you are. You end up making sacrifices just to keep the peace, all the while doubting your worth and wondering how others see you. For more insight, a great resource is Mary Jo Fay's book *When Your "Perfect Partner" Goes Perfectly Wrong.*

I stayed with Jason as long as I did because I was like the frog in slowly boiling water—I kept convincing myself that things were fine. I also realized that only someone with weak boundaries can be manipulated by a narcissist (I'll talk more about that in chapter 4). And honestly, fear kept me stuck. My self-confidence was shot, and I started believing his claims that I couldn't make it on my own. But thankfully, that October night, I trusted my intuition.

Returning to the story, Jason got a new wardrobe, joined a gym, subscribed to a dating app, and had a new girlfriend within a month. Meanwhile, I was being wooed by a sexy guy at work named Luca. He was tall, muscular, and had that rebellious, bad-boy vibe. I fell for him with the urgency of someone gasping for air after being underwater for too long.

But of course, it wasn't really love. I had fallen into a classic pattern described in Abigail Trafford's book *Crazy Time*. The book explains that marriages ending in divorce are often unbalanced, with one partner being dominant and the other more submissive. I was clearly the submissive one. Interestingly, it's often the submissive partner who ends up initiating the divorce, while the dominant one resists it.

To add to the pain of a messy divorce, many people end up going on wild sexual sprees or falling in love quickly, a phenomenon called *coup de foudre*—that sudden "bolt of lightning" feeling or love at first sight. But that spark usually doesn't last, and it can be emotionally draining. This cycle can keep repeating until you decide to take control of your life—by getting healthy, going back to school, starting therapy, and stopping the search for romance to fill the gaps in your life. Of course, that's way easier said than done! *Crazy Time* is an excellent book for anyone who is married, divorced, or remarried. Who knew all of this could be so predictable?

Luca was my coup de foudre. He drew me in by writing these beautiful words while I was separated from my husband:

> I haven't been able to lift my face from the muck for some time, it's been encrusted by the sun, frost, droughts, and floods...that is, until I met you. It took some time for us to connect with all the obstacles, but you must know that I've been your biggest fan since day one. Faith and belief aren't just words in the dictionary; they're concepts that govern life and love. But so is fear. I appreciate your patience with me as well, I have so much passion for you that is lying in wait; for there is a small thread of consciousness in my mind telling me not to feel so much because it might be all for not. That's fear. You must know that I believe in you first...the fear is a tiny sliver. More importantly, I have faith in you but not at your expense. The last thing I would ever want you to do is feel like you had an obligation to not let me down. Like I said earlier, unlike a signed document declaring marriage, I desire love that is unspoken and natural at this moment in time. Thus far, I'm getting a sense of that...I see it in your eyes, hear it in your voice, and feel it in your arms.
>
> I can express how much I think the future would be great if we were together, how much I would love to care and support you, but "that" hasn't happened yet. If you are

confused by all that I am writing, just know that when we are together and when I breathe the same air you breathe so close to you, I am motivated to make you happy in every moment that we share together. This is how I feel about you right now.

I mean, wow, right? It seemed like I was finally getting things figured out. Not even close. Unfortunately, this was my first—but definitely not my last—experience with a guy saying things he didn't mean. Two months later, Luca wanted nothing to do with me. A quiet, whispered "I love you" snuck out during a cozy winter night, just as Jason and I were filing for divorce. That sent Luca running like the house was on fire. (Note: Dating experts often warn women not to say "I love you" first. Most men prefer to be the ones to say it first; otherwise, they feel pressured by the implied commitment and might freak out, even if they do love you.)

Suddenly, Luca wanted space and unkindly blamed me for not giving him what he needed. I was crushed and terrified—now broke and alone. Two years later, he reached out again, wanting to get back together, insisting that we would've worked out if I had just given him more space. It took a few more experiences before I realized that one guy's definition of "space" could be very different from another's.

Attachment Theory, originally developed by psychiatrist John Bowlby after World War II to address the struggles faced by homeless and orphaned children, explains the dynamics of long-term human relationships. In the 1980s, Cindy Hazan and

Phillip Shaver expanded it to adult romantic relationships, identifying four attachment styles: secure, anxious-preoccupied, dismissive-avoidant, and fearful-avoidant.

Securely attached adults have positive views of themselves, their partners, and their relationships. They're comfortable with both intimacy and independence, balancing the two.

Anxious-preoccupied adults crave high levels of intimacy, approval, and responsiveness from their partners, often becoming overly dependent. They tend to be less trusting, have lower self-esteem, and worry more, leading to impulsiveness in their relationships.

Dismissive-avoidant adults prioritize independence and often seem to avoid attachment altogether. They see themselves as self-sufficient and suppress their feelings, dealing with rejection by distancing themselves from their partners, who they often view negatively.

Fearful-avoidant adults have mixed feelings about close relationships—they want emotional closeness but also feel uncomfortable with it. They tend to mistrust their partners and see themselves as unworthy, suppressing their emotions and seeking less intimacy.

Luca was dismissive-avoidant. According to various researchers, relationships with avoidant types are often the most difficult and least satisfying. Although my relationship with Luca was painful and confusing, I was lucky that he cut off any attempts I made to reconnect. Other avoidant types are happy to drag things out, even though there's rarely a future with them.

Luca wasn't just my coup de foudre; he was also like the rocket that gets a spacecraft out of Earth's gravity field. Once the spacecraft is free, the rocket is released—it's no longer needed. This analogy stems from an oldie but a goodie, *How Did I Get Here?* by Barbara DeAngelis. In her book, DeAngelis explores the idea that certain people, circumstances, and even parts of ourselves play a role in our journey but are meant to be let go as we move on to new stages in life. This insightful book has brought comfort to many of my loved ones in different situations. It's definitely worth checking out if your heart is hurting or if you find yourself feeling confused, for any reason.

The end of my whirlwind affair and my marriage was gut wrenching and agonizing. I felt the heartbreak physically, as if it were coursing through every part of me. Normally, stress makes me overeat—chocolate, bread, cheese, pizza, ice cream—you name it. But this time, I couldn't eat at all. I was shaky, barely able to breathe as I stood outside the house I was about to rent from Ed, who later became one of my closest friends.

The Friday night before I moved out and into my new place, I sat in my school psychology class, tears welling up in my eyes. I'm not usually one to cry easily, but this time, I couldn't hold it in. My professor noticed and asked if I was okay. Instead of answering, a choked sound escaped my throat, and tears streamed down my face in front of all my classmates. I hurried to the restroom, where a friend followed me and offered comfort until I could pull myself together.

At thirty-one, I felt like an outsider, having been married and living in the suburbs while my classmates enjoyed downtown life together. That night, they convinced me to join them at a bar. I ended up getting drunk and meeting a charming twenty-eight-year-old guy who loved to text. It was a brief fling, but it provided the distraction I desperately needed.

The next day, nursing a hangover, I drove with my dad to pack up my things from the old house. Jason was there when I arrived, and his parting words stung: "Be careful out there," as if he doubted my ability to take care of myself. Saying goodbye to two of our three dogs felt like a heavy blow to my stomach and chest. While it was a small consolation that Jessie, our remaining dog, would be happier as an only pet, I prayed Jason would take good care of the others. As my dad and I drove away, tears streamed down my face.

That night, sitting alone in my new home, I felt terrified and shaken by the sudden changes in my life. My mom comforted me as I cried once more. Somehow, I managed to fall asleep, and the next morning, I focused on simply breathing and taking things one step at a time.

I found solace in long, slow walks with Jessie around the cemetery near my new place—strangely fitting, yet oddly comforting.

Unexpected Gifts from the Starter Marriage

Today, I feel a deep sense of gratitude for my ex-husband. Life's most challenging relationships often teach us the most profound lessons about ourselves. My time with Jason showed me how easy it is to fall into unhealthy patterns that seem to meet emotional needs but ultimately chip away at our self-worth. Recognizing toxic behaviors—like narcissism—is key to breaking free from those cycles. Trusting your intuition, even when it feels scary, is often the first step toward reclaiming your life.

After leaving a dysfunctional relationship, it's natural to feel lost or even fall into familiar mistakes in new relationships. Healing, however, comes through reflection and making better choices over time. In relationships, healthy attracts healthy. By understanding your patterns, reconnecting with your inner voice, and giving yourself the grace to heal, you'll find your way toward balance and self-love.

Take time to reflect and reconnect with your inherent worth. You matter in this world. Scientists say the odds of you being born are about 1 in 400 trillion—a statistical miracle. Your life has purpose and immense potential. Don't let anyone diminish that. Use your experiences to learn, grow, and do good. And maybe have a little compassion for the difficult people in your life—they're likely struggling in their own way.

Don't let anyone else define your worth. You are enough just as you are.

Personal growth often comes from the hardest experiences. Even if you feel like the frog in boiling water, unaware of how bad things have gotten, there's always a way out. Trust yourself, lean on those who care about you, and take one step at a time.

Love

Love is like war: easy to begin but very hard to stop.

—H. L. Mencken

That summer, while still working at the same place as Luca—which was far from enjoyable—I took some classes to keep busy. To distract myself, I joined a few dating apps. I went on so many dates that I lost count, sometimes even fitting in two in one night. In hindsight, I should have been more selective, but after being married to a narcissist, it felt liberating.

The most promising date that summer was with a Mormon guy who'd had a crush on me back in high school. I remember thinking after our first date that he might be "the one" (Note: dating experts often recommend focusing on enjoying the moment rather than immediately picturing a guy as husband material.) We went to a Rockies game, played golf, and took long walks where he shared stories about his loving childhood. There was definitely chemistry, but he was dealing with his own spiritual issues and eventually decided he didn't see a future with me.

As summer came to an end, I still hadn't found anyone I really connected with and was thinking about taking a break from dating. My confidence was still shaky, and the idea of being alone, unsure if or when I'd meet someone again, was pretty intimidating. That's when I started attending my friend's church. Sometimes, I'd sit by myself in the back, lights dimmed, crying and praying to God. Being married to a scientist had left me skeptical about religion. I hadn't grown up going to church regularly and knew embarrassingly little about spirituality, but I found it surprisingly comforting.

I didn't have to stay alone for long. Just two weeks later, as I was starting to find some spiritual comfort, I met two new people. Once again, I found myself trying to fill unmet needs with romance.

One of my dates was with a thirty-four-year-old surgeon. We met for coffee, had a stimulating conversation, and ended the date with a kiss. Meanwhile, an old college acquaintance, Chris, started reaching out to me through Facebook. He was coming to Colorado for a visit. Chris had been my ex-husband's little brother in their fraternity, and we used to double date back in college. I remembered him as a tall, skinny guy, but when I picked him up at his hotel, he greeted me with a warm embrace and twirled me around like we were old friends reunited. Chris worked in insurance but dreamed of starting his own business.

As we walked to the restaurant's patio seating, I felt a sense of pride having him as my "date," even though it wasn't technically a date. Chris had a two-year-old daughter from a previous marriage, but as we talked for hours, our bodies naturally leaned in close. Later, when we moved inside, his brother joined us, and I ended up sitting next to Chris. The closeness was intoxicating. After a warm hug goodbye, Chris called the next day to say he'd had a great time.

Why did he have to live in Oregon? We started emailing and talking on the phone every night, sharing stories and getting to know each other. Chris sent flowers to my work with a note saying "I'm not sure what this is or where it's going, but I'm pretty sure it's positive." I joked that I'd bake him cookies, but instead of mailing them, I could fly out and deliver them myself. He agreed, and I booked a flight to Oregon during my fall break in October.

As for the surgeon, he was a good match on paper: cute, lived in Colorado, had a great job, enjoyed outdoor activities, and took me to nice restaurants. But the emotional connection wasn't there like it was with Chris. Plus, he had a bit of an arrogant streak. Despite this, before my trip to Oregon, I was convinced the surgeon was the better choice. It all seemed so much more practical.

Before my trip, I had a vivid dream where I was on a beach with Chris while an airplane flew overhead, heading back to Colorado. In the dream, I was shouting, "Wait, no! As much as I love this, I need to go back to Colorado. I don't want to stay here." But I had missed the plane.

That dream felt like a clear sign of what was to come. I realized that while love was inevitable, it might not be right for me, and ignoring my intuition would come at a cost.

When I arrived in Portland, our first kiss was spontaneous and sweet. We spent the night together and toured wineries the next morning on our way to Lincoln City. Despite my reservations, being with him was thrilling. Lincoln City, near the ocean, was chilly and windy but romantic. I snapped a photo of him, thinking, "We'll always be good friends, at least."

Back in our hotel room, we enjoyed wine while Chris accidentally flooded the heart-shaped hot tub with bubbles from too much shampoo. He joked, "This qualifies as my fault," and I laughed, imagining him as a great husband. Dizzy from the wine and aching from laughter, I thought, "It can't get better than this."

The rest of the week was just as magical. We visited more wineries, explored Portland, and listened to soft music while it rained outside. Chris told me he loved me and hoped I would fall in love with him and move to Oregon to be with him and his daughter. At the airport, as he sat across from me, doubts began to creep in. He wasn't sure I'd move to Oregon, and he couldn't leave Brittany. But looking into his soulful eyes, I knew I had to be with him.

If my feelings for Chris didn't already make it obvious that things didn't work out with the surgeon, I have a bit more to share on that. To his credit, the surgeon was upfront and told me he had herpes before anything serious happened, but he assured me he was on medication, so if our relationship progressed, everything should be fine. (Just a little reminder to be extra careful out there!) Not long after that, though, he told me he didn't see a future for us. Problem solved.

Three weeks later, Chris flew to Colorado, and I fell even more in love with him. I couldn't get enough of him, like Jessie with bacon. I'd never been so completely happy. While visiting some friends, he asked me, with the cutest expression, if I wanted to be his girlfriend. The answer was obvious, and we began seeing each other every six weeks or so.

That Christmas, I met Chris's ex-wife and daughter. Everything went smoothly, but despite my love for working with kids, I felt a deep sense of fear. I wasn't ready for the complexities of being in a relationship that involved a child and an ex-wife. More than that, I feared he might never be able to love me as fully as I already loved him. Even with all these doubts, I couldn't bring myself to walk away.

By spring, we were trying to figure out when and how I would move to Oregon. I was set to graduate with my school psychology degree in May and was focused on landing my first job. But Oregon's state licensing requirements were different from Colorado's, making things more complicated. Chris kept insisting that it didn't matter if I found a job as a school psychologist—he just wanted me there. After all of my hard work, that didn't sit right with me. On top of that, trusted voices in my life, like my dad, kept telling me I wasn't ready to make such a big commitment yet. I still needed time to air out from my divorce.

During spring break, Chris and I took a road trip through Seattle and enjoyed a quick getaway to Orcas Island. The anticipation of seeing each other was like the exhilarating rush of a roller coaster's first drop—it felt exactly like I had dreamed. But when we returned to his place and Brittany was set to visit the next night, the roller coaster came to a sudden stop, and the reality of our situation hit hard. Anxiety took hold of me, and Chris seemed unaware of my worries, which led to an argument between us. By the time Brittany arrived, I felt like an outsider. I tried to make the best of it, but the constant yearning to be with Chris was wearing me down.

I hadn't found any job leads in Oregon, so when the school district where I did my internship offered me a position, I decided to take it. Chris congratulated me, saying he was proud and happy for me, but I could sense he wasn't thrilled about another year of long distance.

I suggested that we take things slow and not rush into a big commitment, especially since neither of us had been divorced for very long.

That summer, I drove to Oregon with Jessie and spent three incredible weeks with Chris. Just before heading back home, we took a trip to Costco where we found ourselves admiring engagement rings. We stumbled upon a stunning one-carat ring and decided to buy it. Chris proposed to me right there in the Costco parking lot. I was overwhelmed with excitement and certainty about our future together, but I still felt a bit uneasy about making such a huge move. I think I was still working on rebuilding the self-confidence I had lost during my marriage to Jason, and needed the stability of my job and family more than I felt ready to leap into a new life. I was still healing from my past and hesitant to leave the comfort of what was familiar for the unknown. If Chris had understood this better, I might have felt more secure in our decision.

As soon as I got back from Oregon, Jason stormed back into my life with full force, and my migraines made a painful return. I had recently received a substantial IRS check made out to both me in my maiden name and to Jason. During our marriage, I had taken out the maximum student loans on Jason's advice, which we used for living expenses. He and his parents assured me that a trust fund would cover everything after graduation, but since our marriage ended before that, I was left with a hefty student loan to repay. I was determined to figure out if I was entitled to any of this money before handing it over to Jason. (In the end, I chose not to go to court and let the matter go, receiving no compensation for enduring a marriage to a narcissist.)

This time, both of us had lawyers, and things were getting ugly. Jason even threatened to get me fired from my job, accusing me of causing him injustice. The stress was overwhelming. I wanted to turn to Chris for support, but he seemed emotionally distant. It felt like being at a party where you're excited to reconnect with an old friend. You spot them across the room, excitedly make your way over, and just as you start chatting, they abruptly turn and walk away, leaving you standing there, alone and confused.

As the fall and winter passed, Chris and I experienced intense cycles of passion, laughter, and disagreements. The moments we shared felt special: cuddling during movies, taking walks, enjoying mountain views, and his playful habit of licking my face, which always made me laugh. But those cherished moments were fleeting, often giving way to more challenging times. Chris began showing signs of jealously, growing uncomfortable with my friendship with Ed, despite my unwavering commitment to him. It reached the point where I felt obligated to spend my weekends waiting for him.

One April weekend, during a trip to Oregon, I decided to surprise Chris while he was with Brittany. I had flown in to interview for a school psychologist position and wanted to show him how committed I was to making this move. Renting a car, I drove to his place, hoping he'd appreciate the effort. We had a good weekend together, but I found myself shedding a few tears, overwhelmed with the sadness and fear of leaving my home in Colorado. I tried to explain to Chris that my sadness wasn't about him—it was part of my emotional journey. In my heart, I was silently asking, "Please let me feel this, and be there for me. Reassure me that everything will be okay." But to Chris, any trace of sadness seemed like a sign of doubt, and he expected only excitement from me.

Later, Chris said, "I sat with you while you cried. I could have been out with Brittany instead," his tone suggesting, "What more do you want from me?" It made me question if my expectations of a life partner were too high. Looking back now, I realize that fear often led my decisions, and fear rarely produces the best outcomes. Maybe I could have handled things differently.

That spring, Chris sat in my car, his intense eyes locking with mine as he promised he would never intentionally hurt me—and I believed him. He never would. I had landed a school psychologist job and let my current district know I was leaving. Everything seemed set. The job was in Vancouver, Washington, close enough to Portland to make the licensing process easier. Chris supported the plan, even though it meant being farther from Brittany and his work.

After the school year ended, I stayed in Colorado for a bit longer to tie up loose ends—sorting through belongings, packing, spending time with family and friends. Chris didn't voice his feelings then, but he later admitted that he wished I had moved sooner.

One night in June, my mom and I went to the movies, and I accidentally left my phone on silent. Ed came over afterward with his daughter, and in the meantime, Chris had been trying to reach me. When I finally picked up, he didn't believe my explanation and angrily told me not to come to Oregon or Washington. I was stunned and outraged—I had already quit my job in Colorado to be with him. Eventually, he apologized, saying he didn't mean it, and I reluctantly accepted his apology. Deep down, I knew it was immaturity speaking, but the damage was done. The hurt lingered, amplifying my doubts about our decision.

To complicate things further, I had the "brilliant idea" to detour through Yellowstone on my way to Oregon, delaying our new life together by a day. Looking back, maybe it was my last attempt to hold on to a bit of independence before fully diving in. Though I was excited at first, that excitement quickly turned to fear, mixed with a growing sense of resentment. Chris had pressured me, saying that if I didn't move right away, I might lose him. It felt like an impossible choice, but my love for him was strong enough to push through.

I had no idea that Chris saw my delay as a setback to our fresh start. If I had known how much it hurt him, I never would have taken that extra time. Sadly, this miscommunication and the resulting hurt feelings set the tone for what was to come—a rocky start to our journey together.

In July, I arrived in Oregon, eager to reunite with Chris, who was especially tender that afternoon. We decided to keep things low-key for the Fourth of July since we were both exhausted. The next evening, as we settled on the couch and into our new life together, I shared an idea with Chris—a suggestion from my friend in Colorado. She had proposed that since I had summers off, I could visit Colorado with our future kids for a few weeks each summer, giving them time to bond with my parents and Chris's family. It seemed like a reasonable compromise and eased my anxieties about the move, until Chris adamantly declared, "You will never take our kids away from me for two weeks."

Chris's strong reaction stemmed from his own painful divorce experience, where he had limited time with his daughter. Even in calmer conversations afterward, his stance remained firm. What seemed controlling and unfair to me only heightened my anxiety.

Less than a week after my arrival, I celebrated my thirty-fourth birthday. Chris had planned to take the day off so we could hike and enjoy a nice dinner together, but his mind was preoccupied with concerns about renting out his home and finding a new place in Vancouver, Washington, where we intended to live. We spent the day house-hunting instead, which, while pleasant, lacked our usual fun and connection. The evening ended with an unexpected argument after a lovely dinner in Portland. Neither of us could recall what sparked it, but in a moment of stress and frustration, Chris angrily told me to leave his house. Refusing to be pushed around, I stayed the night, but resolved to leave the next day.

As I packed my car and looked for an apartment in Vancouver, Chris called, deeply apologetic. I returned to his house, and that night, we decided to give our relationship another chance—the very reason I had moved there in the first place.

On the way to sign the lease for our new home, another explosive argument erupted, leaving us both bewildered and on edge. Stuck on a bridge in Portland traffic, Chris's stress boiled over, leading to a heated exchange where he expressed desire to get out of the car, and I broke down in tears. The scene was distressing, far from the future we had envisioned.

A few nights later, we argued about money in front of others at Olive Garden. Chris's harsh words stunned me. In hindsight, I realized a healthier response would have been to set a boundary and walk away, refusing to tolerate the disrespect.

As the weeks went by, Chris was constantly juggling work, Brittany's presence, and his father's summer stay in Portland, leaving little time for us to be alone. Whenever I tried to express my needs, Chris grew frustrated, eventually labeling me as a nag. In an effort to avoid conflict, I stopped seeking comfort from him altogether. While this cut down on our arguments, it left me feeling isolated and missing the warm, sensitive man I had fallen in love with. By late July, doubts began to surface—I wasn't sure if I could marry him.

Over the next month, our relationship became a sea of negativity, with only occasional attempts at positivity from either of us. In psychological terms, maintaining a healthy relationship requires a balance of positive and negative interactions, with a ratio of at least five positive exchanges for every negative one—ideally closer to nine. If you're familiar with John Gottman, PhD, and the Gottman Institute, you might know that his research shows successful couples maintain a 5:1 ratio even during conflict and a 20:1 ratio of positive engagement in everyday conversations. On the flip side, factors like criticism, defensiveness, stonewalling, and contempt are strong indicators of relationship breakdown.

While my experience wasn't as scientific as Gottman's studies, it became clear that our relationship had become so heavily skewed toward negativity that it was hard to find a way back. Here are a few examples to illustrate the imbalance in our relationship:

- I tried to comfort Chris when he was upset about moving expenses, but he pushed my hand away and told me to leave him alone (-3).
- He surprised me with Clinique's clarifying lotion, which I appreciated (+1).
- He invited his dad to live with us for eight days without telling me (-1).

- When Chris suggested trading cars for better gas mileage, I refused because I already felt my life was spinning out of control, which led to more tension (-4 or -5).
- One morning, I covered the bathroom with notes listing all the things I loved about him (+1).
- I wore a dress he bought me to dinner with his family, and he complimented me, which made me feel good (+1).
- Chris wasn't thrilled about me joining a running group for the Portland Marathon and voiced his concerns, so I decided not to join (-2).
- We played tennis together once, which was enjoyable (+1).
- When I mentioned that I used to play tennis with my parents at Brittany's age and suggested we could all play more often together, Chris reacted negatively, which hurt (-1).
- I needed help putting up a fence for Jessie, and Chris grew frustrated, ripping part of the bush and yelling at me (-1).
- Our cat accidentally got outside, leading to a heated argument where Chris accused me of leaving the door open on purpose and being selfish (-1). I tried to express my feelings with an "I" message (+1), but he insisted he was just stating the truth (-2).
- When Jessie lightly snapped at Brittany, Chris reacted by hitting Jessie, which deeply disturbed me (-5).

- During a weekend with Brittany, I chose to go hiking alone with Jessie instead of joining in on family swim time, which caused some conflict (-3).
- Chris bought me a $15 shirt at Costco (+1), but later criticized me for not considering his financial situation before allowing him to buy it (-3).
- He bought chicken for dinner, and I made a healthy meal most nights, contributing to our household (+1).
- Chris requested to see my grocery receipts to ensure I was contributing more than just rice, which felt intrusive and led to tension (-3).
- In a hurtful moment, Chris calmly told me that I would never have a child as good as Brittany, which deeply upset me (-5).

In total, there were seven positives against thirty-four negatives. To get out of that slump, we would have needed at least 170 more positives (34 × 5), which was a drastic step neither of us was in the mood for.

These conflicts persisted, leading to the return of my migraines. The Sunday before Thanksgiving, Chris broke up with me again, leaving me with a knot in my stomach. Desperate for an escape, I left the house for a bit, finding comfort in a conversation with my friend Tyler, who pointed out several signs that maybe it was time for me to return to Colorado:

- My mom had been laid off from her job.
- My previous school district had offered to rehire me.
- I had my first panic attack at the grocery store.

I returned home with a new sense of confidence and determination. Chris noticed the shift in my attitude and started flirting, drawing me back in despite my growing doubts.

Thanksgiving only brought more tension. Chris failed to tell me that Brittany wouldn't be arriving until later, which frustrated me since I had already invited a friend to join us for dinner.

His solution was to take Brittany out separately for Thanksgiving, leaving me feeling excluded and hurt. Although we eventually shared dinner together, my mom observed a noticeable lack of affection between us that weekend.

After Thanksgiving, Chris seemed to relax, which coincided with me taking on most of the financial responsibilities. Despite my lingering attraction to him, his demeanor had grown colder, and I found it increasingly difficult to trust him. By December, I had interviewed with my old school district in Colorado and received a job offer. I was faced with one of the hardest decisions of my life: should I trust Chris and risk my career and emotional well-being for our relationship, or should I return home? In the end, I chose to go back to Colorado.

Ironically, once I made that decision, our relationship seemed to improve. We spent time playing games, celebrating Christmas with Brittany, and reconnecting. On Christmas morning, I dropped Chris off at the airport as he headed to Florida to see his family, leaving me in a state of numb disbelief. Spending Christmas alone, I began packing, getting ready for the drive home with my dad and Jessie.

Unexpected Gifts from Love

My time with Chris was a rollercoaster of emotions and tough choices, all while I was trying to find my own stability and happiness. Looking back, it was a real eye-opener about what it takes to build a healthy relationship and maintain personal growth. Here's what I learned:

- **Put your well-being first:** Always make sure your decisions, especially about relationships, support your own mental and emotional health.
- **Be honest and open:** Good communication is key. Make time for real conversations where you both listen and understand each other's feelings. Use "I" statements to share how you feel without placing blame.
- **Reflect on yourself:** Use tough times to learn about what you need and want. This self-awareness helps you make better choices and avoid past mistakes.
- **Balance your independence and commitment:** Find a sweet spot between keeping your own identity and being invested in the relationship. It's important for lasting happiness.

- **Get your life in order:** Before making big changes, make sure you have a solid base to support them. Stability in your life helps strengthen your relationship.
- **Don't rush:** Take your time with big commitments. Address your own emotional baggage before jumping into a new relationship.
- **Face your fears:** Acknowledge your fears and get support if needed. Respond to your relationship challenges in a healthy way.
- **Know your worth:** Set boundaries that reflect your values and self-respect. Don't be afraid to speak up for yourself.
- **Take care of yourself:** Focus of self-care—get enough sleep, eat well, exercise, enjoy nature, and appreciate life's small joys.
- **Forgive and move on:** Let go of grudges, whether they're toward yourself or your partner. Forgiveness is crucial for healing and keeping old wounds from reopening.

If you're looking for more advice on healthy relationships, check out John Gottman's *The Seven Principles for Making a Marriage Work*. His book is packed with great tips for building strong, lasting connections.

Life after Love

When one door of happiness closes, another opens; but often we look so long at the closed door that we do not see the one that has been opened for us.

—Helen Keller

By January 1st, I was back living with my mom, dealing with a storm of emotions: overwhelmed, relieved, depressed, confused, guilty, worried, and angry. Adjusting to new schools as an early-career school psychologist was already tough enough—I felt like I was just learning to walk again after navigating an emotional battlefield. On top of that, I was diving into the exciting process of searching for a new house to buy.

There was talk of Chris maybe moving to Colorado, but he ended up choosing Seattle instead. In January, he visited Colorado with Brittany to see his family, and even though we still had emotional ties, our relationship continued to suffer. He came back for another visit in March, but we ended up arguing again. After a tearful goodbye at his family's house, before he left for the airport, I watched him in my rearview mirror until he faded from sight—that was the last time I saw him.

My heart was still tangled up with Chris, but my mentor and best friend, Anna, saw what I couldn't. "This isn't healthy," she said. "You need counseling. I know a great counselor."

Enter Evelyn Williams—a tall, striking woman in her fifties with short, blondish hair. Her office had a calming vibe, but she commanded respect from everyone, even high-powered attorneys and self-absorbed individuals. She quickly became my guiding force, much like Richard from Texas to Liz Gilbert in *Eat, Pray, Love*.

From day one, Evelyn urged me to "let go. You've acknowledged that your mom, dad, Anna, Tyler, and Ed all saw this wasn't good for you, right?" she asked.

"Yes," I replied.

"Well, you need to let go. It's like driving forward while constantly looking in the rearview mirror—you'll never truly move on that way."

"I know," I murmured, grasping the concept but unsure how to practically let go and survive.

I put my trust in Evelyn and in the advice of those around me, even more than in my own instincts. Gradually, and with some reluctance, I began to let Chris drift away. We still talked, but less often. It was painful, and I had regrets for a while, but this was the start of my healing journey. I found some comfort in reruns of *Sex and the City*, trying to convince myself that everything would turn out okay eventually.

Taking Evelyn's advice, I started journaling my feelings and practicing gratitude. I tried out different coping strategies, like getting massages and joining group spiritual activities. These were meant to shift my energy, as the Taoists would say.

While these strategies helped, one thing became clear: time was the biggest factor. Just like physical injuries need time to heal, emotional wounds need patience. For those of us who like to get things done quickly, I learned the hard way that rushing the healing process only leads to frustration. Healing takes as long as it needs to, and no one should rush you with clichés like, "You should be over this by now," or formulas suggesting, "It takes half the time of the relationship to get over him." Allowing yourself this time is crucial for gaining perspective and moving forward with a clearer mind and emotional balance.

Night after night, I lay in bed next to Jessie, wondering if the pain would ever ease up. During May and June, I poured my thoughts about Chris into my journal while cautiously dipping my toes into the dating scene, despite Evelyn's wise advice that I needed more time to heal. In hindsight, she was right—it was too soon, but I didn't realize it at the time.

An attorney I knew took me out on five dates, only to end up with someone else. To show me there were other possibilities, my dad introduced me to a twenty-eight-year-old golf pro at a Nuggets basketball game. He pursued me for two and a half months, gradually winning me over. We spent evenings listening to music in the back of his truck, went to concerts in the rain at Red Rocks, and enjoyed cookouts with his friends. We played pool at dive bars, went camping, and shared moments that felt like the beginnings of something special. He was open about his feelings, saying things like, "I'm falling hard for you, is that okay?" and "I haven't felt this way about anyone in a long time." He even declared, "I'm in love with you."

This experience got me thinking about Steve Harvey's ninety-day rule, which suggests taking time before diving in emotionally. But just as I started to lower my guard after two and a half months, he disappeared. Despite his claims of love and various excuses—busy schedules, inconvenient distances—I knew something was off. The letdown was even harder to handle with my thirty-fifth birthday approaching.

My birthday was a stark reminder of my heartache. With no plans and a heavy heart, even simple tasks felt like a burden. Despite everything, I mustered the energy to throw myself a birthday party, trying to avoid feeling irrelevant.

In mid-July, I took a trip to Washington, DC to visit an old friend, hoping for some comfort. Although my heart still hurt and my steps felt slow, the getaway offered a brief break from my emotional haze. Exploring the city gave me moments of peace, helping me remember Chris while also seeking clarity for what's next.

Returning to school in early August felt like stepping into a new chapter—a recovery phase that often felt more like a performance than real progress. For the first time, I faced an uncertain future without a clear plan. As someone who's always been a planner, this shift was unsettling. I was grappling with big questions about wanting kids and finding lasting love. Even though my dad suggested taking time for myself and Evelyn recommended waiting two years, I found it tough to balance my desire for companionship with the need for personal growth.

Eventually, I realized that solitude is a valuable gift. It's a chance to reconnect with yourself and address things you might have ignored. While loneliness can be tough, it's also time for reflection and self-acceptance, crucial for personal growth. It's an opportunity to reclaim your independence and explore what you enjoy without compromise. As Barbara DeAngelis puts it, it's a moment to ask, "What am I free to do now?"—a chance to embrace rather than fear, knowing it's just a temporary phase.

Ultimately, embracing solitude helps us set healthy boundaries and build self-awareness. When we really get to know and accept ourselves, we can approach new relationships more authentically, without putting on masks or making compromises. It's about finding emotional stability and true happiness within ourselves, so any future love can be built on a solid foundation of honesty and mutual respect.

Reflecting on events from a year ago, it struck me how surreal it was that Chris and I had once planned a life together, yet now existed worlds apart. Anything remotely connected to Oregon or Washington—a work article, a glimpse of the Seattle skyline on *Grey's Anatomy*—stung with memories. I used to know every detail of Chris's daily routine—his sleep schedule to his gym habits. Now, all I knew of him was the skyline on TV Thursday nights.

Despite my efforts to stay positive and surround myself with uplifting people, the clichés of well-meaning friends started to wear thin. Phrases like "You have to be happy on your own first" and "It'll happen when you least expect it" became frustratingly common. I couldn't count how many times I'd heard these lines, and I wasn't the only one who found them unhelpful.

For those of us navigating singlehood, genuine empathy and encouragement meant much more than canned advice.

In late August, I reluctantly agreed to attend an eight-minute dating event with a friend. The experience was disappointing; most of the men seemed socially awkward and older, far from what I hoped for in someone who could spark a connection. But in the midst of all this, there was a silver lining. Ethan, an old classmate from middle and high school, recognized me at the event. We exchanged numbers and soon found ourselves having long conversations over dinner. Though we were both still healing—him from a broken engagement, and me from Chris—we decided to give dating a shot, but it ended up being too soon for both of us.

One night, I had a powerful dream where I was driving to Oregon and Camas, Washington, but without Chris. The whole thing left me with a bittersweet feeling about what could've been. The lush scenery and horses seemed to symbolize a missed opportunity, while the barren, difficult return to Colorado felt like a metaphor for the emotional journey my heart was enduring.

Evelyn, my counselor, painted Chris as a narcissist, comparing him to my ex-husband, just in a different way. Still, the thought of "You had your chance" kept replaying in my head.

Evelyn suggested I had a pattern of attracting controlling men, hinting that maybe there were deeper issues within myself that I hadn't fully come to terms with yet.

In therapy, I learned how unhealthy attachments can blur the line between real love and something more like addiction or infatuation. Evelyn gave me a handout that broke down these differences: Toxic intimacy can show up as an obsession with finding "someone to love" and the need for instant gratification. This can lead to pressuring a partner for sex or commitment, creating an imbalance where control and manipulation take over. In these kinds of relationships, trust is often shaky, and one or both partners may try to change the other to meet their own needs. These relationships tend to be built on fantasy, ignoring the real issues, with the hope that one partner will somehow "fix" or rescue the other. It's easy to confuse passion with fear, and both people can end up blaming themselves or each other, leading to a frustrating cycle of despair.

Healthy intimacy, on the other hand, is all about building a strong sense of self first.

In these relationships, there's a focus on long-term happiness, and connections form gradually. Both partners respect each other's freedom, and the relationship has a balanced give-and-take, where compromise and shared leadership are the norm.

Communication is honest and open, and trust comes from really understanding each other. Instead of trying to change one another, each person appreciates the other's individuality, allowing the relationship to grow naturally from genuine friendship and care. When problems arise, they're tackled together, creating a positive cycle of comfort and happiness.

I realized I had a lot to learn and unlearn on my path to emotional health and real intimacy.

Over a span of two and a half years, I cycled through the five stages of grief—denial, anger, bargaining, depression, and acceptance—over and over, and in no particular order. Grief, I found, is a very personal journey that doesn't follow any set timeline. Some move through it quickly, while for others, like me, it takes time and feels like it drags on forever.

Grief isn't just about losing someone to death. It's tied to any big change or separation—like the end of a relationship, a new phase in life, or even major transitions like kids leaving home or retirement. It shows up in all kinds of ways.

That fall, my emotions were all over the place—denial, depression, anger, and bargaining—but acceptance still felt out of reach. I wrote in my journal:

> I can't get him out of my head. It's been months since we last talked, but he's on my mind every day (depression). Why is my heart so slow to catch up with my head? If he really cared like he said, wouldn't he be here by now instead of in Seattle? (anger). I still hope he'll realize his

mistakes, apologize, and come back to me because he loves me (denial). Ed said it took him over a year to move on from someone he loved.

I miss Chris—the way he made me laugh, his energy, the way he loved me (when he did), his eyes, his touch, his voice—everything. He moved me in ways I can't explain. When will this ache go away? God, give me strength and healing (depression). I feel like I'm making progress, but I know I'll never be the same. Thank you, God, for the things that bring me comfort: my family, Jessie, Evelyn, my work, my home, books, health, and friends, even *Sex and the City*.

I'm grieving not just the thought of never seeing him or Brittany again, but also the future I imagined. A breakup like this, at this stage of life, feels so devastating (depression). It's not just losing him; it's losing the dream of the life I thought I'd have.

By the end of September, I reached out to Chris (bargaining), hoping for some kind of movie-like reunion where he'd realize his mistake and come back to me (denial). But reality didn't match my hopes. He was distant on the call, talking fondly about his new life in Seattle. It was clear he had moved on, and for the first time, he didn't end the conversation with "I love you." That hit me hard. I felt a deep emptiness, realizing he had chosen Seattle over me and moved forward without looking back. The pain was overwhelming, and I hated myself for hurting so much (depression).

I prayed to God to help ease my pain, stop obsessing over him, and find real happiness again. Even though I was cycling through these stages of grief, depression seemed to have a strong grip on me. That's why I leaned on psychological strategies for dealing with depression, which helped build resilience. Resilience is about having flexible responses—cognitive, behavioral, and emotional—to tough times, and at the heart of it is your attitude.

Evelyn suggested finding a church or similar community that matched my beliefs, but instead, I joined a running club and tennis league. I wanted to focus on my strengths while pushing myself outside my comfort zone to build resilience. The key is to find something you're passionate about and connect regularly with people who share those same interests.

One of the strategies that really helped me build resilience was "learned optimism." It's about retraining your mind to shift from negative, pessimistic thinking to more positive and productive thoughts. Back in the 1990s, psychologist Martin Seligman and his team studied people who thrived despite facing adversity. They found that optimism—viewing things with a positive outlook—was closely linked to resilience and success in tough situations, while pessimism often led to depression and feelings of helplessness. Seligman's work ultimately showed that optimism isn't just something you're born with—it's a skill you can learn, and it can make all the difference when life gets hard. Seligman found that optimism is a powerful tool for coping with adversity and preventing depression, and he proved that optimism can be learned. He showed that pessimists can shift to a more optimistic outlook—not by faking happiness but by developing new ways of thinking.

In his work, like the book *Learned Optimism*, Seligman introduced techniques for tackling negative thoughts. These strategies include identifying problem situations and then challenging irrational beliefs, considering their consequences, and actively rethinking negative thoughts with more balanced ones. For example, instead of thinking "Nobody loves me," you might reframe it to recognize that while not everyone shows love the same way, there are people in your life, like family, who care deeply. This practice builds a more resilient and positive mindset.

Spirituality has also been a big help for me in dealing with depression. My Christian beliefs, along with insights from Buddhism and Taoism, have shown me the importance of acceptance, letting go of attachments, and keeping a positive mindset despite life's challenges.

Buddhism, founded by Siddhartha Gautama (the Buddha) around 2,500 years ago, explores the purpose of life and its inherent suffering. Buddha taught that suffering comes from clinging to desires for pleasure and material things, which distract us from understanding the true nature of existence.

Buddhist teachings suggest that happiness and despair start in our minds. True happiness and relief from suffering come from training our minds, changing how we see ourselves, and improving our relationships through our thoughts and words.

Life's challenges are seen as chances for growth. Embracing difficulties and showing love, even to those who hurt us, can help us heal. Negative emotions like anger harm us, while love promotes well-being. Forgiveness is key to self-acceptance and letting go of past hurts.

The Buddha taught that living in the present and not getting stuck in the past or worrying about the future helps us find stability and freedom.

Taoism, founded by Lao Tzu in the sixth century BCE, has had a big impact on Chinese culture. It focuses on living in harmony with nature and letting things unfold naturally to find peace. It teaches that our thoughts and words are powerful. According to Taoist ideas, focusing on positive aspects of life connects us with a greater sense of harmony, while dwelling on failures can lead to more problems.

Taoism also suggests that our thoughts shape our experiences, much like how modern physics shows that our observations can influence the behavior of particles. In essence, our attitudes and emotions impact our lives and the world around us.

Our interactions with others show just how connected we all are. We share energy with those around us, and this can either lift us up or drag us down. People who feel disconnected from their own energy might end up drawing from others, which can change these dynamics.

Even though these ideas are inspiring, I struggled with the practical side of things: How do I find peace when I'm in so much pain?" Even with daily meditation, my impulses often got the better of me. The best strategy I came up with was to repeat positive phrases every day and stick notes in visible places to remind myself that I could get through it. It took a lot of discipline and time, much like sticking to a diet.

Not ready to let go, I decided to email Chris in a last-ditch effort to ease the pain I was feeling. This led to a phone call where I couldn't help but smile when he accidentally called me "Sweetie" out of habit. He also sent me a heartfelt email saying, "I will always have love for you, but I'm not sure I'll ever be able to move." Even after that, he continued to text me now and then. For months I found myself obsessively checking my email and phone, clinging to the hope of hearing from him.

By October, I was still stuck on what could have been. The sadness wouldn't lift, and I kept questioning myself:

- Was it my fault for struggling with the situation?
- Did I ruin something before it even had a chance to start?
- Could he have loved me but stopped because of me?

My dad offered some perspective saying, "Chris didn't truly love you; it was infatuation for him. If the timing had been right, it would have just taken longer to fall apart. He needs to mature, and that could take years. Plus, real change is pretty rare." Hearing this from my dad, my counselor, and everyone else made me wonder if I had tried hard enough and if it was finally time to let go.

Still seeking to ease my pain in all the wrong ways, I felt like I needed to be more proactive by late October. Worried about what everyone, especially my dad, would think, I emailed Chris to address his comment about not being able to move. He called me right away and said, "I think about you every day too. It wouldn't be any time soon, but maybe I could move back to Colorado. Things aren't going that great for me in Seattle." The door wasn't completely shut, and I couldn't help but feel a bit hopeful.

In November and early December, things with Chris seemed to be looking up. He called me occasionally, and we exchanged emails regularly like we used to. He called me beautiful and sent me loving messages just like before. But by mid-December, he started pulling away, and I couldn't figure out why. My mom and I went to Mexico for Christmas, and I found myself missing Chris and the life we had hoped for. I didn't hear from him during Christmas or New Year's. When I texted him "Happy New Year," he replied, but it felt different.

Noticing something was off, I sent him an email saying I wasn't sure I could keep going with this. His response was basically just an "Okay," which sent me into a deep depression. I called Evelyn for an emergency session because I knew it was really over. Once again, I couldn't eat or sleep, and my eyes teared up regularly at work. Who had I become?

I decided to start training for a spring marathon, and somehow, that gave me the strength to keep going. It gave me a new focus and was the only thing I knew to do. It felt like something I needed to do. So there I was, facing my huge fear of the unknown. Just as I was about to take that scary leap into something new, I met Paul.

Unexpected Gifts from Life after Love

Heartbreak, while painful, can bring unexpected and powerful benefits. It acts as a wake-up call, urging you to rethink what truly matters and what you genuinely desire in life. For me, heartbreak taught me patience and self-compassion. It showed me how to navigate the difficult process of letting go and made me realize the importance of understanding and expressing my emotions—something I needed to work on. This experience opened me up to new possibilities and helped me become more aware of the blessings in my life. Often, the most meaningful growth happens during the transition from crisis to recovery.

Think about how a pearl forms: an irritant gets inside an oyster, and in response, the oyster secretes a fluid that layers over the irritant until a beautiful pearl is created. Our healing processes works in a similar way, building layer by layer, leading to deep growth. The wisdom gained through this hard-fought journey is invaluable, a beauty that can't be achieved any other way.

The pain, disappointment, and despair I experienced allowed me to connect more deeply with others, as loss is a shared human experience. Heartbreak brings greater compassion, courage, and self-confidence because you survive what you thought you couldn't. It creates space for new possibilities, often better than what you imagined, and sparks creativity.

If I were to offer advice to a friend going through a broken heart, here are the suggestions I would give (if asked, of course!):

- **Embrace your heartache:** Allow yourself to feel your emotions and process the grief. Don't push your emotions away, at least not all the time. Notice if you start overloading yourself with busyness, jumping into new relationships, or using substances more—these might be signs that you're avoiding the healing process. Facing your feelings head-on can help you heal faster. If you're feeling stuck, consider seeking help from a mental health professional.
- **Cope in healthy ways:** Journal, talk to supportive people, exercise, clean your space, eat healthy (at least most of the time), watch a funny movie, read a good book, and make sure you're getting enough sleep. Remember, winter has to pass before spring can arrive.
- **Be mindful of your language:** The way we think shapes how we feel and act. Use empowering language. Instead of seeing your relationship as a failure, view it as a valuable learning experience.
- **Focus on love:** Notice the love you receive from others. Focus on your best qualities and what you have to offer. Acknowledge the good in your ex. Give love where you can—to a pet, a garden, or through acts of kindness.

By approaching heartbreak with openness and resilience, you can transform it into a powerful force for personal growth.

Third Time's a Charm?

Success consists of going from failure to failure without loss of enthusiasm.

—Winston Churchill

In January, I attended a wine-tasting event with a girlfriend and met Paul. He was a handsome, forty-eight-year-old recently divorced vice president of finance for a large corporation in Denver. Paul was the type of polished man who regularly wore suits to work. He was tall with azure eyes and a touch of gray in his hair, giving him a distinguished look. Buoyed by the generous pours of wine, I felt confident and flirty that evening and initiated our new relationship. Nevertheless, Paul began courting me.

He took me to upscale downtown restaurants and always picked up the tab, a pleasant change from Chris. We attended art walks, charity art benefits, symphony performances, and even visited a Chinese massage parlor. Paul had perfect manners, was thoughtful, and treated me like a queen. It was so easy and so different. Is this what it was like to date an emotionally mature man? I could get used to this! While it didn't have the same passion and laughter I felt with Chris, with Paul, I felt safe. He understood me, and if we ever got upset with each other, we could work things out calmly and rationally.

During spring break, we flew to Las Vegas, drank a lot, and had a good time. We always drank a lot, as if we needed it to loosen up around each other. When we returned, Paul started talking about taking a trip to Central America together. I couldn't believe it: a man actually wanting and able to take me on a real vacation. In June, we escaped to a foreign country for ten days. It was surprisingly easy being with him during that time. We started off in the city, where a lovely lady approached us and told us about her long-lost love. Paul's Spanish-speaking ability was quite appealing. We meandered through local towns, visiting some of his friends, and ended up in a beautiful beach house, where a monkey greeted us, sleeping in a chair on our porch.

One sunny afternoon on the beach, we were relaxing and drinking. Paul wanted to take a picture of us using the timer on his camera. The camera fell, and I didn't realize the picture didn't take. At that moment, I saw some dogs running on the beach and wanted to pet them—I was missing Jessie, after all. I motioned for Paul to join me, but he didn't. When I walked back, Paul was already packing up and leaving. I called for him, but he didn't hear me. By the time I gathered my belongings, Paul had taken the car and left. I had no idea where he went.

I waited for a while at our beach house and then decided to take a shower. It was then that Paul burst in and yelled at me for not locking the door. I was confused and frightened. Paul was upset because I ran off to see the dogs before we finished taking pictures. He felt hurt that I didn't seem to appreciate our relationship and special time together. I was upset that he didn't talk to me or tell me where he was going and then barged into the bathroom to yell at me when I was vulnerable. We worked it out, but this was the first sign our relationship wasn't as perfect and mature as it seemed.

When we returned home, we had a gala to attend for Paul's work. I was tired from traveling and not in the mood to go, but Paul handled my annoyance gracefully, which warmed my heart. Watching him that night, confident and sure of himself in his work setting, was enticing. Things were back on track, and by July, I was deliriously happy, especially when we had friends over for dinner, and it felt like we were a real couple. However, I had to admit that although I felt very close to Paul, I still didn't feel the certainty I once felt with Chris.

It felt like I had promised my whole heart to Chris somewhere along the way. It felt like he was running around Seattle with a piece of my heart, and I didn't know how to get it back. I prayed to God to help me let go and grow that missing piece of my heart back. As much as I tried to deny this lingering truth, Paul must have sensed it, because once I returned to work in August, things began to crumble.

Love has a way of bringing out our deepest fears and insecurities, exposing those false core beliefs we hold onto. For Paul, those beliefs—skewed ideas that affect how we see relationships—were about to come into full play. Charlotte Kasl, PhD, sums it up well in *If the Buddha Dated*: "There are two basic emotions—love and fear. When we feel love, we are free of fear, and when we feel fear, we are unable to love." With Paul, there were moments when it felt like pure freedom—light, open, and safe. But then fear would creep in, tightening its grip.

Kasl goes on to say that when we're not feeling love, we get stuck in confusion or an illusion. And I think that's what started happening between us. False beliefs in relationships are like filters, making us see rejection or fear intimacy when there's no real reason to. They make us sabotage things, project our insecurities onto each other, or constantly look for reassurance. The problem is, no amount of validation is ever enough when the belief itself is broken.

My perfect, mature, easygoing boyfriend, who made me feel safe and accepted, suddenly turned into, dare I say, a whiny, needy, inconsolable adolescent. It began when Paul handed me an article about opposite-sex friends and relationships. Apparently, Paul was still upset about my having dinner with my friend and colleague Tyler in March and the fact that I sat next to Tyler while talking to several friends at my birthday party. Paul and I tried to create a relationship agreement to handle these situations. I was perturbed that it took him so long to share his annoyances with me. It felt dishonest somehow.

Our phone calls became exasperating. There were long, awkward silences where he waited for me to initiate, respond, or react in a certain way. He regularly waited for me to say, "I love you," before saying it himself.

On Thursday, July 29th, I wrote:

> He's perfect in so many ways—fun, sweet, and thoughtful—but I feel like he struggles with emotional intimacy. Something just feels off. He's too reserved, holding back, and always following my lead instead of being fully present. Even after all this time, he reacts to me and watches me to decide how to act. I try to be compassionate and reassuring, but it doesn't seem to be enough. He says he's being himself, and I believe him, but I think he doesn't fully know or trust himself in relationships. He's so focused on doing the right thing that he's not just being, which makes things less fun. We aren't connecting emotionally or laughing much.

Saturday, August 21st:

> Paul actually said we could have a family together one day. He provides everything that Chris couldn't: time,

compassion, career stability. I know that Chris is long gone and never coming back, but I still haven't reconciled what exactly happened. My fear, timing, immaturity, narcissism? My counselor always says I'm addicted to the controlling narcissism. But maybe I'm just addicted to the love. That kind of love, healthy or not, is addicting to the human brain. And, for me anyway, without that love comes less fear, less need to control, and less passion. Maybe that's just real life? Am I the one getting in the way of true love, or am I still trying to fit a square peg in a round hole?

Sunday, August 22nd:
Any time I ask for something I need from Paul—however small—he thinks it relates to our relationship. For instance, a night to myself to get work done or getting off the phone after 'only' twenty minutes because I'm in the middle of writing reports. I made an effort to be especially nice about it. Maybe he senses I'm not 100 percent in love with him and he feels insecure? I do love him. Love is so abstract, so many different kinds, yet all the same. Haven't people been asking that question for ages—what is love? How do you know if you're in love?

My big question right now is how much faith to have and trust that everything will work out okay—or how much depends on my decisions? I don't want to make any more big decisions, because so far the worst-case scenario always seems to occur. And if left up to faith, nothing may ever happen. Are all the philosophies real, or are they cultural and man-made to survive?

Paul—I want so much to have the chemistry with him. We're missing the laughter; he self-deprecates almost all the time, and he's insecure until I spend an hour on the phone comforting him. I want to be in love with him. He's such a good person. He's thoughtful, kind, consistent, cute, and he can afford to take me out. What do I do?

A few weeks later, at the end of September, we attended another fancy event. The evening was enjoyable until I stepped outside the ballroom around 10:00 p.m. to get some water. Checking my phone, I saw a text from Tyler asking to borrow my ladder. I replied with a joke about asking for a ladder at 10:00 p.m. on a Saturday night and went back inside. Thinking it was funny and wanting to be forthright, I shared the story with Paul, remembering the handout he gave me during the summer about being open in our relationship. Paul's mood shifted, and he exploded during the car ride home, accusing me of breaking a rule and suggesting Tyler wanted to sleep with me. That ended the night on a sour note.

The following Friday night, we spent hours on the phone. Initially, Paul was silent, then he wouldn't stop talking about how little time we spent together, despite our consistent twice-a-week meetings. He didn't seem to understand the struggle I faced balancing work and our relationship. My efforts to meet the demands of both were exhausting, and it felt like my best wasn't enough. Yet we must have reconciled, as the next day we enjoyed my dad's birthday celebration.

At the beginning of October, Paul had a "breakthrough." He realized his trust and attachment issues stemmed from his childhood, acknowledging that nothing I did would have ever been enough. He promised to change. The man who once described himself as Mr. Spock from *Star Trek*, who hadn't cried in twenty years, now cried—on my couch, as we parted, and on the phone.

Despite his promises, the issues persisted. Paul was determined to see only what he wanted, making communication and resolution difficult. My boundaries were weak. When I mentioned needing weeknights to myself for work, Paul suggested he'd still come over but make it comfortable, like every day. He dismissed my concern that it was hard to work with him around, implying his solution was "our" solution. I felt selfish and rigid, doubting my worth as a girlfriend, even though my needs were valid. He wouldn't problem solve with me, only for me. When I raised concerns about our interactions, he'd simply deny them, resolving the issue for himself but not for me. His constant crying and focus on his issues became exhausting, resembling my work routine, and left me feeling guilty, frustrated, and utterly worn out.

As the "wackiness" continued, despite his promises, I suffered four migraines in one week. It seemed men were giving me migraines. Louise L. Hay's book, *You Can Heal Your Life*, suggests that physical ailments often stem from unresolved past issues and negative beliefs. Migraines, for example, indicate "resisting the flow of life"—perhaps trying to force relationships that aren't meant to be? The new thought pattern to alleviate migraines is "I relax into the flow of life and let life provide all that I need easily and comfortably. Life is for me." Interestingly, after Chris and I broke up, he complained of kidney problems, which Hay suggests indicates "Criticism, disappointment, failure. Shame. Reacting like a little kid." One of my mom's worst eczema bouts occurred when I lived with Chris, and eczema's probable cause is "breath-taking antagonism. Mental eruptions."

Amid my headaches and confusion, my dad advised, "Wait until fall break, get rested, and then see how you feel." He still believed I wasn't ready for a real relationship. My mom said, "If you follow your heart, it will take you to the right place." Evelyn remarked, "Your biggest strength is also your biggest weakness: loyalty."

One Friday night in October, while working on reports at home, I received an email advertising a free three-day trial on Match.com. Restless, I signed up, curious to see what might be out there if Paul and I broke up. He was everything I wanted, yet doubt and frustration gnawed at me. What harm could a free three-day trial do?

The next evening, Paul came over, and we ordered dinner, but I soon fell ill and fell asleep. (Vomiting equals violent rejection of ideas; fear of the new.) My "perfect, mature, easygoing" boyfriend seized the moment to go through my phone, accessing all my emails and texts, discovering my Match.com profile. He denied snooping, claiming he found me on Match.com by chance.

Furious, I terminated the free trial. I felt guilty, initially ignoring his breach of trust in going through my phone. It was evident from the emails in my trash folder that he had snooped. Despite his denial, the look on his face told me he was lying. Eventually, he confessed, but somehow, I ended up being the villain.

The following Saturday, I reluctantly joined Paul at the couples' counselor he had suggested. Her name was Mindy, and I immediately liked her. She had a presence that felt both wise and fair. Sensing my frustration and exhaustion, Mindy suggested a two-week break, a terrifying prospect for Paul but a refreshing respite for me. I spent the break going to a Halloween party with friends, attending church with my mom, doing yoga and meditation, catching up on work, reading, sleeping, and spending quality time with Jessie. It was blissfully peaceful.

As my two weeks of freedom were winding down, I went downtown with an acquaintance named Matt and met some of his friends. It wasn't as fun as it might have been in my twenties; it was downright depressing. A nearly fifty-year-old man monopolized me all night, leaving me no chance to meet any attractive guys. One girl, thirty-five, was still hung up on her college sweetheart but had married and divorced someone else. Now, she was likely to have a baby on her own within the year. Another woman, thirty-nine, was still waiting to meet someone special. A sweet, homely thirty three-year-old pursued Matt, though he wasn't interested. Another girl in her thirties kept dating men who came on strong then bailed after three months. If this is what being single at thirty-six means, I might just stick to Netflix with Jessie and call it a night.

That same night, Paul showed up at my house in a cab, drunk, thinking it was romantic. We were still on a break, and I was annoyed. I stayed calm, let him stay the night, and drove him back to his car in the morning. Both counselors, Evelyn and Mindy, confirmed that his behavior was selfish and ignored my needs. I still had no boundaries. The proper response would have been to not answer the door or call another cab without worrying about the cost.

Ah, boundaries—such an important topic that keeps coming up. Let's delve into it. According to *Boundaries* by Dr. Henry Cloud and Dr. John Townsend, boundaries are what help us keep the good in and the bad out. Without them, life can leave us feeling isolated, helpless, confused, and guilty, like everything's spinning out of control. Trying harder, taking on other people's problems, and ignoring our own needs won't fix it. What works is taking ownership of our lives, and boundaries are key to that. It's about knowing what's ours to handle and what isn't.

Cloud and Townsend describe four common boundary problems. First, there are "Compliants"—people who say yes to things they shouldn't, often out of fear of hurting someone's feelings, being abandoned, facing anger, or dealing with shame. They give into guilt and let a harsh inner voice guide them. Then there are "Avoidants," who say no to the good stuff. They struggle to ask for help, recognize their needs, or let others in. When they're in need, they withdraw, mistaking boundaries for walls. But healthy boundaries should be like fences with gates, letting in the good and keeping out the bad. Those who put up walls end up shutting out everything—good or bad.

Next are the "Controllers," who don't respect others' boundaries and try to manage their lives by controlling others. There are two types: "Aggressive Controllers," who bulldoze over others' boundaries, often being verbally or physically pushy. They try to mold others to fit their own view of the world, ignoring the need to accept people as they are. "Manipulative Controllers" are sneakier, using guilt trips or persuasion to get others to comply, subtly twisting situations to their advantage.

Lastly, there are the "Nonresponsives," who don't recognize or respond to others' needs. They neglect their responsibilities in relationships, tuning out the needs of those around them and failing to offer the care and support that's needed.

On a Saturday night in November, Paul and I had planned to enjoy a ceramics class together. However, the evening took an unexpected turn when I attempted to set a boundary. I wanted to spend time with him but didn't want to stay the night for two reasons: 1) it eats up half of my Sunday, and I miss my run, and 2) I had a big presentation to prepare for on Monday morning. In trying to communicate my true needs, Paul became very upset. He cried all night, we argued, he almost broke up with me, and he even told me I would end up alone forever.

We never made it to the ceramics class. I felt like a hostage in his car because Jessie was locked inside his house. His thoughts were so irrational that I oscillated between feeling extremely angry and immensely guilty. Mindy, our couples counselor, later suggested that I should have given Paul more notice about not staying the night. I agreed, but my fear of conflict—a compliant boundary problem—held me back. However, Paul should have accepted my decision. In a relationship, both people need to enthusiastically agree on an activity. Since I wasn't enthusiastic about spending the night, we shouldn't have done it. Paul struggled to understand that my self-sacrifice for his wants and needs was ultimately destroying our relationship. His love bank was full, but mine was depleted.

Over the Thanksgiving holiday, Paul and I spent three nights together, and things were finally better, even enjoyable. By mid-December, though, Paul developed a pattern of calling me each night, becoming upset, and then sending long, multipage emails the next day. The source of his frustration was a Facebook picture of me and my friend Tom at my birthday party before I even knew Paul. I deleted old pictures on Facebook, but Tom still had that one, which Paul took as a sign that Tom wanted to sleep with me. Paul insisted, "You are naive, and it's hardwired in me by evolution; any other guy would feel the same." He claimed he was just following Mindy's advice to get everything out in the open. "Why can't you understand me?" he asked.

One Saturday night, I prepared a nice dinner for Paul and me. Yet again, we had to talk about our issues. I felt like I didn't even want to be around him anymore and attempted to discuss breaking up, noting that we hadn't been happy for months. Paul wouldn't let the Tom issue go, so I finally called Tom to confirm we were just friends. I felt mortified but was desperate for Paul to stop obsessing over it. Suddenly, the issue that had upset Paul for months seemed resolved. He proclaimed that everything would be better now (a sentiment I had heard before). He said I was the love of his life, talked about me being cute when pregnant, wanting three kids, what kind of engagement ring I wanted, and how happy we could be. I told him I wasn't ready for that yet. When he asked when I would be, I said we needed more time to see if we could just be happy.

Evelyn grew increasingly worried about my relationship with Paul. She said, "Pushing for marriage is a very big red flag. Marriage would only make things worse for you. You have a chance to be happy. You would benefit from some time alone to really get to know yourself and help with your boundaries."

Evelyn opened my eyes to the warning signs of a controlling personality, which can sometimes escalate into something more dangerous. While I never thought Paul would become abusive, it's important to be aware that this can happen. If a person shows three or more of these behaviors, there's a strong chance that the situation could become physically violent:

- **Jealousy:** Often mistaken for love, jealousy is really a sign of possessiveness and lack of trust. A partner might question who you talk to, accuse you of flirting, get jealous of time spent with friends, family, or children, call frequently during the day, or drop by unexpectedly.

- **Controlling behavior:** This often starts off as concern for your safety or decision-making, but can turn into anger if you're "late" or if they question where you went or who you talked to.
- **Quick involvement:** Pushing for marriage, engagement, or living together within six months of meeting, saying things like, "You're the only person I can talk to; I've never felt loved like this by anyone." They pressure you to commit quickly, making you feel guilty or like you're "letting them down" if you want to slow down.
- **Unrealistic expectations:** Expecting you to meet all their needs and be the perfect partner, with lines like, "If you love me, I'm all you need. You're all I need."
- **Isolation:** Accusing your friends and family of "causing trouble," and trying to cut you off from your support system.
- **Blaming others for problems:** Almost anything that goes wrong is somehow your fault.
- **Blaming others for feelings:** They might say, "You make me mad" or "You're hurting me by not doing what I want."
- **Hypersensitivity:** Easily insulted and claiming their feelings are "hurt" when they're actually very angry, often ranting about perceived injustices.
- **Cruelty to animals or children**
- **"Playful" use of force in sex**

- **Verbal abuse:** Making degrading remarks, cursing, or belittling your accomplishments, or telling you that you're stupid and can't function without them.
- **Rigid sex roles:** Expecting you to serve them without question.
- **Dr. Jekyll and Mr. Hyde:** Sudden mood swings, going from nice to explosive in an instant.
- **Past battering:** A history of violent behavior.
- **Threats of violence**
- **Breaking or striking objects**
- **Any use of force during an argument**

Evelyn also taught me about the mind games controlling personalities often play, including:

- **Lies**
- **Excuses**
- **Blaming**
- **Shaming**
- **Vague information:** Making facts and details unclear and confusing.
- **Double messages:** Sending positive message followed by critical ones, or saying one thing while doing another.
- **Failure setup:** Manipulating you into actions that guarantee failure, which they then use to control you.
- **Image making:** Treating you more like an object or a role than a person.

- **Mental invasion:** Telling you or others what you're thinking or feeling.
- **Faulty interpretation:** Acting as if you said something you didn't.
- **Distracting:** Changing the subject or focus during a confrontation.
- **Exaggerating:** Blowing things out of proportion.
- **Confusing the issue:** Overloading you with information to obscure the real point or pressuring you to make decisions when you're overwhelmed.
- **Promises:** Offering something important if you comply, but never delivering.
- **Degrading:** Using "teasing," sarcasm, or verbal attacks that make you feel ignorant, incompetent, or childlike.
- **Guilting:** Interrogating you until you feel the need to apologize constantly.
- **Distrust:** Constant questioning, accusations, and shifting the focus onto you instead of them.
- **Jealousy, anger, and distrust:** Disliking the people who are important to you, punishing behavior, acting sullen, withdrawing, giving you the silent treatment, and blaming you for everything.

The dysfunctional ways people often respond to these mind games include:

- Not confronting or questioning the behavior

- Compromising your own needs and boundaries
- Trying to please and appease them
- Giving the silent treatment
- Playing nurse or caretaker
- Falling into chronic self-doubt and overanalyzing everything
- Acting out fear of abandonment or rejection

Recognizing these behaviors and responses is the first step in breaking free from their control.

Evelyn helped me recognize these controlling behaviors, mind games, and my dysfunctional responses that had occurred in all of my relationships. I realized I needed to break this pattern to have a chance at being happy and healthy in a relationship. This awareness led me to wonder, "How did I develop this toxic pattern in my romantic relationships?"

In *The Nice Girl Syndrome* by Beverly Engel, the author outlines four main roots of "Nice Girl" behavior, which includes both women and men who often find themselves in controlling relationships with weak boundaries. The first origin is biological predisposition, where someone is naturally inclined to be patient, compassionate, and more focused on maintaining connections rather than engaging in confrontation. The second origin is societal beliefs, which are passed down by the culture or society in which one grows up. Girls are often taught to be polite, agreeable, and pleasant, molding them into the Nice Girl persona.

The third origin, familial beliefs, comes from family influences, either through direct teaching or by observing family members. For example, having a passive mother, growing up in an ultraconservative or deeply religious family where women are considered second-class citizens, or being raised in a misogynistic environment can all contribute to this pattern. The final origin is experiential beliefs, which are shaped by personal experiences, often involving trauma. Many Nice Girls have endured physical, emotional, or sexual abuse either in childhood or as adults, which reinforces their Nice Girl behavior.

Engel also dives into the top ten reasons, beyond these four main sources, why women tend to be too nice. These include fears of not being liked, fears that others won't be nice to them, fear of confrontation, fear of rejection or abandonment, and fear of being ostracized from their social circle. Additionally, Nice Girls might fear feeling their own anger, becoming like an abusive parent, being perceived as too masculine, or being labeled as a "bitch" or "ball-breaker." They also worry that if they aren't nice, men won't protect or provide for them.

The book explores how fear is a common thread in Nice Girls and offers guidance on transforming these false beliefs into empowering ones. It provides strategies for developing confidence, competence, conviction, and courage. The *Nice Girl Syndrome* is an excellent resource, especially if you see yourself in the patterns described.

Neuropsychologists explain that the reason we unconsciously repeat certain patterns is similar to Engel's idea. When we are young, before our brains are fully developed, we often go through situations where a negative gets stuck in our minds and etched into our hearts. This happens because, as kids, we can't always grasp the reality of what's happening, so we create a negative belief about ourselves to make sense of it. For example, if a child struggles in school and receives a lot of criticism, they might think, "I'm not smart enough. I'll never be good at anything." As adults, we know that struggling in school doesn't define someone's intelligence or potential, but a child might internalize that belief and carry it into adulthood.

As adults, we might unknowingly gravitate toward people, places, or situations that reinforce these negative beliefs as a way to heal and break free from them. It's like our mind is giving us a chance to say, "I'm not buying into that anymore because the truth is I am a good person and I deserve to be happy." We'll keep repeating the pattern until we finally heal and embrace the truth about ourselves—that we are good, worthy, smart, strong, capable of success, deserving of happiness, love, health, or whatever it is we need to believe.

How hard can it be to put theory into practice, anyway?

A few days before Christmas, I was feeling so discontent that it was driving me crazy. *Boundaries* by Cloud and Townsend explains that real love can't thrive without boundaries—otherwise our love might just stem from compliance or guilt. I was starting to realize that I wasn't in this relationship for the right reasons (for all *The Bachelor* fans out there!). On top of that, I was completely drained, a clear sign that I wasn't in sync with my own flow or energy. Despite this, I gathered the courage to try the breakup speech once more on a cold winter evening while we sat in Paul's car. As expected, he pushed back, and I wavered. "Everything is different now," he said. "We've worked things out. Please, we haven't had any normal time together, and it's Christmas. We're supposed to go to the mountains!" We had planned to spend a few days in the mountains skiing, but I wasn't up for it and told Paul so. This led to more tears and pleading, and I ended up giving in. This mix of looming conflict, subtle manipulation, and my own tender emotions wore me down. Looking back, I question what I was so afraid of. So, we went to the mountains and had a nice time, but we cut the trip short because of the dogs.

Paul was disappointed we didn't stay longer, but he didn't make a big deal about it this time.

In January, Paul started planning for spring break and found a great deal for a week-long trip to Costa Rica. I hesitated, which puzzled him because, in his mind, who wouldn't want to go to Costa Rica? At first I wasn't sure myself, but my hesitation was due to my busy job, and the thought of spending the entire spring break away felt overwhelming. I suggested that while I'd be happy to go somewhere for part of the break, I also wanted a few days to relax at home. This didn't make sense to Paul for a couple of reasons: 1) it seemed financially impractical to go somewhere else for a shorter period, and 2) if I didn't want exactly what he wanted, he assumed it meant I didn't love him enough.

Mindy, our couples counselor, gave the same verdict as before: although I could hear my own needs, I crumbled quickly due to my fear of conflict and guilt. As a result, I tried to please by taking responsibility for things that weren't mine to handle. Paul, on the other hand, needed to grasp the difference between compromise and manipulation. He didn't understand—or agree—because he believed his intentions were good. Paul was incredibly skilled at manipulation, and it felt like I was being repeatedly hit over the head with the same issue in my relationships. If I didn't address it soon, I was in serious trouble.

One Saturday night in mid-January, Paul and I were actually having fun. We went to dinner and then joined my friends at a Nuggets basketball game. That night, Paul was drinking, and I was not. At one point, I disagreed with him about something he shared with his personal counselor that I thought was meant to be private between us. He shut down completely. I tried to lighten the mood with humor because, honestly, it wasn't a big deal to me, but he refused to talk to me for the rest of the game and the drive back to his house. He became completely irrational, reverting to his erratic behavior, crying and making a scene. I did my best to reassure him, set a boundary, and then I left.

In *Boundaries* by Cloud and Townsend, they explain that one of the first signs you're starting to set boundaries is experiencing feelings of resentment, frustration, or anger in response to both subtle and overt violations in your life. Just as radar detects an approaching missile, your anger can signal that your boundaries are being crossed.

He, of course, didn't sleep at all that night, and somehow that was my fault too. There were so many obvious attempts at manipulation and guilt. The next day, he came over to my house and even tracked me down at the grocery store. While he was more rational than the night before, he still wasn't entirely composed. When I chose not to engage with his "discussions," he accused me of putting up a wall. However, according to *Boundaries*, not engaging is actually an appropriate response. By Sunday, he admitted to acting childish and seemed to expect that everything would be magically forgotten.

When I discussed Paul's behavior (i.e., manipulations) with Evelyn, she said, "You've said he pouts when he wants to do something 'nice' for you, and you say, 'no thank you, not right now.' He projects onto you, saying, 'Nothing is wrong with me. I'm a good partner. I only need a little bit from you because I'm the anxious type. I think you're the avoidant type.' He thinks all your problems would be solved if you lived together and saw each other every day, which is actually an attempt to make you responsible for filling a void for him. He has control/emotional immaturity issues that probably won't go away." It was beginning to sink in, but I was still hesitant to trust myself. Yes, after all that I'd been through up to this point, I was only now finally starting to get it.

In January, we celebrated our anniversary. In an effort to enjoy myself and make our relationship fun, I drank too much. Paul took this as a sign that everything was great and my drunken state was my "true" state, only it wasn't. On what planet is it a good sign when one person has to drink in order to have fun with the other?

Then, the Friday before the Super Bowl, having the day off from work, my mom and I had gone snowshoeing and ended up at my house that evening. My mom was in my office and noticed Paul's email open on my computer. My mom suggested that I might learn something if I went through it. At first, I thought I couldn't invade his privacy the way he invaded mine a few months before. But then, my devil side argued that he started it, so I began to read. And found a whole other can of worms.

That can of worms was named Becky. Paul fell in love with Becky while they were both married. Despite Paul's claims of no contact, I found recent and past emails between them. In September, he wrote, "Maybe my sadness comes out with you because we can't be together." In January, he wrote, "I still think of you every day. I miss you and miss talking to you."

I contacted Becky, who shared her side of the story, along with Paul's rebuttals. They undoubtedly loved each other. They met at work, had a brief affair, and broke it off out of guilt. A few months later, Paul told Becky he wanted to spend his life with her, but she chose to work on her marriage. Becky eventually left her job to avoid Paul, but he insisted on weekly lunches. Despite no physical relationship, Paul professed his love, making Becky feel guilty while he rationalized it as friendship.

When Becky tried to distance herself, Paul became extremely depressed and missed work. He'd say he didn't belong on this planet and wished he could give up, blaming Becky for his behavior. Paul denied any suicidal talk and work absences, arguing that he wouldn't have been chosen for his job from eighty candidates if he were suicidal and depressed. Becky continued to see him out of guilt, but Paul maintained they were just friends.

When Paul started dating me, Becky was upset because he never stopped telling her he loved her. She told Paul they couldn't be in each other's lives, but he thought they were just friends. Becky considered changing her life for him but ultimately decided it was too late. Paul disagreed and kept pursuing her. Becky eventually decided to stop seeing Paul, but he continued to contact her, professing love while dating me. Paul denied any wrongdoing, insisting they were just friends. Despite Becky's clarity that they were "lovers who did not have sex," Paul saw her as an important friend.

Occasionally, Paul still contacted Becky, thinking she was still his friend. During his depressive episodes, he reached out to her, struggling to understand why she distanced herself. He told her he thought about her every day and felt more connected to her than anyone else. He asked her, "What is wrong with me? Why doesn't anyone want to be around me? How could you end up hating me so much when I wanted the opposite?" Paul admitted he couldn't understand because they were such good friends.

In the end, Paul insisted that he and Becky were just friends, struggled to understand why Becky didn't want to stay friends, and couldn't grasp why I was so frustrated in our relationship. This was the final straw for me. While he was a good person, he was emotionally tangled up, and we had both been weak in handling things. I ended the relationship on Super Bowl Sunday.

The first few weeks after our breakup were incredibly freeing. I felt a sense of peace and optimism, even with Valentine's Day around the corner. I had decided to take a break from thinking about men or dating for at least three months. Embracing my singleness and freedom, I followed the advice from the Tao books and felt, happy, strong, and confident. That is, until early March, when I received an email from Chris.

"Can we talk tonight?" it said.

Of course we could talk! My first thought was that it was going to be just like in the movies and he was coming back to me. But then I thought more realistically. That evening, just after returning from a run, the phone rang. The sound of his voice sent shivers down my spine. I felt nervous as we exchanged cordial small talk. Then a pause.

"I guess I should tell you why I'm calling," he said. Another pause.

Without hesitating, I replied, "You're getting married, aren't you?"

"Yes," he said.

"Oh, when?" I asked.

"April 16. We've been together for over a year."

"Wow...well, I'm happy for you. I guess I did the right thing by leaving."

"We might have worked out. I'd like to stay in touch with you if that's okay with you."

"You want to be friends? I don't know..."

"Friends sounds so juvenile. But we could stay in touch? Or do you never want to hear from me again? Give you some time?"

"Well...uh...we could stay in touch. That would be all right." With that, we awkwardly wished each other well and hung up, both knowing that phone call was probably the last communication we would ever have.

Tears instantly streamed down my face. In a moment like this, who else would you call but your mom? She came right over, wrapped me in a comforting hug, and stayed with me while I cried—again. It felt as if my body was weighed down by a fifty-pound brick on each limb.

I called in sick to work the next day. Chris was about to enter the safety and security of marriage, while I was utterly single and left with no other choice than a dating app? To make matters worse, my mom found out he was marrying an attorney. He was clearly moving up in the world. Meanwhile, I felt like I was destined to live out my days alone in my tiny house, with no family to miss me when I was gone. How much more could I possibly endure?

Luckily, my newfound freedom led me to join a running club, and the combination of exercise and new friendships kept me moving forward, both literally and figuratively. On the day of Chris's wedding, my mom and I treated ourselves to facials and a dinner out, where we indulged in plenty of wine.

That week, I attended an Access Consciousness meetup—something I had heard about from a coworker. Founded by Gary Douglas, Access Consciousness aims to clear away unhelpful clutter and help people think about life in new, positive ways. As the group leader explained, "Consciousness is the ability to be present in your life in every moment, without judgment of yourself or others. It's about receiving everything, rejecting nothing, and creating everything you desire in life—greater than what you currently have and more than you can imagine." We were encouraged to constantly ask ourselves, "How can this be better?"—a concept similar to the Law of Attraction. While I'm not sure I fully experienced the clearing the leader did for us, I did find myself breaking down in front of the group, just as I had in a class years before. The support from the group was incredibly comforting, and I felt grateful for their presence. However, I had to step away from the group when my summer tennis league started on the same night as the meetups.

I also made two vision boards. The first one was about what I wanted in my life. I cut out pictures and words from magazines and glued them onto a piece of cardboard. I included a couple falling in love and getting married, a group of friends having dinner, a joke to remind me to laugh, a map of Italy, etc.

I also made a man vision board. I listed everything I wanted in a man. I asked a friend who had made a vision board how long it took her dreams to come true. "Not that long. Three years," she replied. Three years? Ugh. Later, I discovered a book called *Soul Vision* by Phoenix Djukic and Cornelia Schwarz, which offered insights on connecting with the true desires of your soul and creating a vision board that works.

I consulted two psychics. One said my next boyfriend would be thirty-eight years old and that my purpose in life was to spread light. The other beautifully described that I was ending a long seven- to fourteen-year cycle and the Universe was removing things from my life that I had outgrown. She advised me not to dwell on old pictures, to be accepting and gracious, and to recognize that I didn't need the past to move forward. It's a season of fall, she explained, and while winter must end before spring arrives, spring will come. Try to understand the beauty. My new love would be simple and understated—slow, practical, and not flashy. He would be older, like a big brother, traditional, religious, educated, financially stable, and a bit of a jester. The last time I talked to this psychic, she said I would marry a person in the legal profession who was very close with his mother.

The things one will reach for when floundering.

Unexpected Gifts from Third Time's a Charm?

Experiencing a relationship while you're becoming more aware of your patterns and fears is a true gift. It's like the difference between taking a class and doing an internship—you don't just learn, you *live* it. While putting new skills into practice can be nerve-racking, the fear begins to lessen once you do—even when things don't go smoothly. My relationship with Paul was a clear example. It allowed me to see my own dysfunction, try different approaches, and observe the results. It helped me conquer (or at least lessen) my fear of conflict and abandonment. Most importantly, it showed me that saying, "No, this isn't for me," isn't as terrifying as I once thought. My negative thought patterns were lies. The truth? I could trust myself more than I realized.

Getting a handle on your relationship patterns and fears is like gaining a backstage pass to your own emotional journey. It's not always easy, but the rewards are worth it. With every small step forward, you learn to trust yourself more and feel more at peace along the way. Here are a few things I've learned that might help you too:

- **Set clear boundaries:** Good relationships need boundaries. Be upfront about what you need and where your limits are, and make sure there's respect on both sides. Without that, things can quickly turn frustrating and exhausting.
- **Look for emotional compatibility:** A relationship might look great on the surface, but emotional compatibility is key. Feeling safe and respected is just the start—you also need mutual understanding. It that's missing, don't ignore it.
- **Focus on self-awareness:** Understanding your own patterns is huge. It leads to better decisions and healthier relationships. The more you know yourself, the more you can grow.
- **Balance love and self-care:** Real love involves respect and balance. Taking care of yourself is just as important as nurturing the relationship. Compromise shouldn't mean sacrificing your well-being.
- **Try new ways to grow:** Be open to different methods of personal growth, whether it's through community groups, vision boards, or advice from others. Staying curious about new tools and ideas can bring a lot of clarity.

- **Embrace change:** Change is part of the growth process. Recognizing that new beginnings can be beautiful helps you handle transitions with a more positive mindset.
- **Ask for help when you need it:** There's no shame in reaching out for support when you're feeling lost. Whether it's advice from family and professionals or exploring new ideas, getting help can be really empowering.

The Revolving Door

A wise woman puts a grain of sugar into everything she says to a man, and takes a grain of salt with everything he says to her.

—Helen Rowland (1875–1950),
American journalist and humorist.

Though my three-month break from men wasn't quite over, I felt restless and decided my search must go on. I joined a few online dating sites and apps to get started.

To kick things off on the right foot, I attended an Instant Attraction workshop by Dr. Jenn Oikle. There I learned that, "On average, one out of every ten people you meet will form a connection with you." A friend's friend found "the one" after meeting twelve people through Tinder, so maybe there's some truth to that statistic. Dr. Jenn taught us how to connect with someone's heart by discussing passions and feelings and how to deliver the Goodbye Sandwich. The Goodbye Sandwich was particularly helpful: it involves sandwiching the news between two pieces of positive information, such as, "I had a great time getting to know you. You're a lot of fun, but I don't think we're a perfect match. I know you'll find someone great, and I wish you the best."

Kevin: I wasn't particularly drawn to his profile, but he "nudged" me, so I gave it a shot. He was short, in his midforties, and had a bit of a smug vibe. We met for a dog walk in the park, and to my surprise, he was cuter than I expected, and we had a pretty nice time. At the end of the walk, he hugged me and said, "It was nice to meet you." And that was it—I never heard from him again.

Gary: Gary was tall, forty-three, and a self-professed goofball who had never been married. He was fun to be around and a great conversationalist. We went out four times—met at the Apple store, went dancing, attended my marathon expo followed by shopping and dinner, and then went dancing again. He was into me because of the "caveman theory," which, according to him, meant I made him feel like a man—mainly due to my size. He liked that I'm five foot two and, oddly enough, was into my ribs (I never quite got that one). In the end, I just wasn't feeling the connection I needed for a relationship, so I gave him the Goodbye Sandwich. Gary took it well, and we even played tennis later as friends.

Shane: A thirty-six-year-old finance guy, new to town. My first impression? Not as cute as his pictures, but I decided to have fun anyway. He took me out to dinner, and he seemed really nice and funny. I decided I liked him—and that's usually when things start to go downhill.

We texted the next day, and he invited me over for pizza and a movie. He kissed me goodnight, and for a moment, I saw some real boyfriend potential!

The next week, I had a tennis event, and Shane suggested meeting up beforehand. He had just come from a financial planning meeting, and somehow the conversation shifted to my finances. Let me tell you—this is a definite no-no early on. Ladies, never, ever talk about your finances to a man, especially in the early stages of dating. After learning I had a student loan and wasn't saving much for retirement, Shane lectured me. "You're thirty-six! You should have been saving for retirement since your twenties."

Then the conversation shifted to tennis. Shane was great at it, but I had been struggling with losing streaks and was feeling down. He pointed out, "You don't talk very confidently about tennis," which only made me feel worse. I tried to save it by saying I am very confident when it comes to marathon running, but by then, it was too late. I never heard from him again. Another lesson learned: act confident, breathe, and relax. Fake it until you make it.

Phil: A thirty-four-year-old professional. We met at a coffee shop, and I accidentally called him the wrong name and asked if he was Shane. Oops. Way to make a first impression. We had a nice conversation, but that was that.

Toby: A forty-year-old professionally scattered dog lover, shy, Mark Wahlberg look-alike. We met for a dog walk at the park and got dessert afterward. Usually, that is a good sign, but I never heard from him again either, even after sending a thank you.

Matt: A thirty-seven-year-old, divorced, no-children, socially awkward engineer. We met for drinks. He acted interested, suggested a second date, but never followed up.

Glenn: A hefty forty-something divorced father and workaholic. We met for lunch, he generously paid, and did all the talking. He suggested getting together for a hike the following Sunday, but when I followed up, he said he was busy and would call later, but never did.

Henry: A thirty-seven-year-old divorced dad and Army guy. He invited me to an Army black-tie event, and since I didn't have any other plans, I decided to go for it. Before the event, we met for coffee and a dog walk. Henry was reserved, but he was smart, well-educated, nice, and somewhat funny.

After our coffee date, though, he started bombarding me with texts, including "Your eyes are really pretty." After date number two, he pointed out that I accept compliments but don't give them and asked for reassurance that I would have enough time for him. Hmm—he was reminding me of Paul.

We had a pleasant time at the black-tie event, but I ended up giving him the Goodbye Sandwich.

Connor: A thirty-six-year-old, single, educated, manager of a hospital problem-solving something. We met for happy hour. He was cute in a boyish way; he talked the entire time, split the check, kissed me goodbye, and mentioned a next time. For our second date, he took me to an expensive restaurant and paid. I did notice he had to blow into a breathalyzer before starting his car. Again, he talked all through dinner without asking me a single question. We kissed goodnight, and he offered to take me and Jessie for a boat ride that weekend. It was a great day, and he made dinner that night. Then it all fizzled out.

Sebastian: On my tenth date, still asking the Universe, "How can this be better?" I met Sebastian. At six-foot-three, he was just as tall as Chris, but with bigger, stronger muscles. On top of that, Sebastian had a law degree from a prestigious university, but instead of practicing law, he was an entrepreneur. Charming, funny, and able to cook—Sebastian seemed to have it all. He was thirty-eight years old (the psychic did say I would be with a thirty-eight-year-old!), divorced, no kids, and loved dogs.

We met on a warm summer evening in mid-June at a patio bar near downtown. His friends were still hanging out when I arrived, but I walked in confidently and quickly hit it off with them. Sebastian bought me a beer, and there was an immediate connection. After his friends left, we stayed behind and talked. That's when he opened up about his romantic history.

When he was younger, he fell in love with two women who, according to him, weren't the healthiest in relationships. Eventually, he married someone he thought was "the right kind of girl" to settle down with. While they had a great relationship, the intimacy disappeared during the last three years of their marriage, leading to their divorce. Not long after, he fell for another woman he believed was "the one," but she turned out to be mean at times and broke up with him via text just six months before we met.

The psychologist in me thought that Sebastian wasn't going to like me. He seemed to have a pattern of falling for the crazies and drama queens, and six months wasn't much time to heal from his last breakup. But my running friends reassured me, saying not to overthink it—people grow and change, and he could very well end up liking me.

When Sebastian offered to cook shrimp scampi for our second date, I was all in. We talked and sipped wine while he cooked, and we laughed throughout dinner. Afterward, he opened up and shared a childhood story that he had never told anyone—not even his ex-wife.

If you've ever read *How to Talk to Anyone* by Leil Lowndes, you know that one way to build a connection is by making someone feel special, like they're the only person you'd share something with. Sebastian was smooth—he knew exactly what he was doing.

After dinner, we settled in on the couch, and Sebastian showed me some of the theatrical work and short films he had directed. My college girlfriends had warned me that theater guys could be a bit eccentric, but the evening was too romantic to let that thought bother me. I melted when he held my hand and told me he really enjoyed my company. In a perfect moment, he leaned in to kiss me. After I left, he texted, "Thank you for a lovely evening." Maybe my luck was finally changing...

Since we were both going to be out of town soon, Sebastian wanted to see me the very next night. He came over to my house, slightly flustered from having trouble finding it. To help him unwind, we sat outside, enjoyed some wine, and talked before dinner. The conversation wasn't as magical as the night before, but we still shared a kiss, and I felt a strong connection. Later in the week, Sebastian called and invited me to a rodeo in Greeley for the Fourth of July.

By the time we returned to Denver, we had been in touch every day since we'd first met. Sebastian came over to my place again, and we spent the evening enjoying pizza, wine, and a movie. He was funny and thoughtful, and we snuggled comfortably. Even though I couldn't shake the feeling that he might be almost too perfect, I refused to let fear control my feelings. For the first time in two and a half years, he truly excited me.

One Friday night in early July, Sebastian and I kicked off the evening at a wine-tasting party, where we held hands and mingled with ease. Later, we joined four of his friends for dinner, and our affectionate behavior made us seem like a well-established couple. However, when two of the guys began discussing work, Sebastian's demeanor changed. He stiffened and cut them off, saying, "I don't want to talk about work. I think about it all day and just want to have a good time," with a slight eye roll. The table fell silent, and I was momentarily taken aback. After giving him a moment, I subtly reassured him with a quiet comment. Gradually, he relaxed, and we went on to enjoy the rest of the evening at Lakeside Amusement Park.

At the end of the night, Sebastian invited me to his work event the next day, but I already had plans to attend a Rockies baseball game. We spoke on the phone afterward, and he came across as unusually curt before abruptly hanging up, which left me confused. He quickly called back to apologize, explaining that he was exhausted from an eleven-hour workday and not much sleep. I offered to bring him lunch the next day, but he seemed more eager to see me than to eat.

During lunch, Sebastian invited me to his parents' condo in Estes Park for the night, which was on the way to the Greeley rodeo for the Fourth of July the next day. He assured me there would be no pressure and thought it would be nice to get out of town. The drive up was fun and comfortable, and when we arrived, he cooked a delicious steak dinner on the grill. We watched a movie and cuddled, eventually heading to bed around 3:00 a.m. I lay next to him, unsure of what might happen. We started kissing, but things, well, didn't quite go as planned. As a regular reader of Cosmo, I knew not to take it personally or make a big deal of it.

That morning, Sebastian made eggs benedict for breakfast, and we were as affectionate as ever. We drove to Greeley, enjoyed the rodeo, and afterward, he showed me around his hometown and all the landmarks of his childhood. That evening, we joined his friends for a Fourth of July barbecue. Sebastian openly treated me as his girlfriend, and made plans for us to go to an outdoor movie on my upcoming birthday weekend. As we said goodnight under the warm summer sky, he told me, "My friends love you. And you're so pretty. I like you." I replied, "That's good because I like you," hoping this could be the start of something special.

The next day, we texted as usual. I went out with girlfriends to Canvas and Cocktails and, when I got home, sent Sebastian a message: "Still up?"

He replied, "Yes." In hindsight, I should have texted, "Want to chat?" instead of calling him. The conversation was strained. His responses were curt and confrontational. For example, when I asked how long he had stayed at his friends' place the night before, he snapped, "Their names are Maggie and Brian. Why don't you use their names? They're your friends too now. Did you forget their names? It's Maggie and Brian." Then he abruptly said, "I'm tired of this conversation, and I'm going to go," practically hanging up on me.

After that, I didn't hear from Sebastian again. Following Evelyn's advice, I gave him space, and two days later, I texted him: "Hi, it seems like something came up the other night. If you'd like to talk about it sometime, I'm open to that. Hope you're well." Four hours later, he responded with a barrage of hurtful messages, criticizing my intimacy and saying he didn't want to continue dating.

As my thirty-seventh birthday approached with no plans in sight, I initially felt a bit down. However, this year, I decided to embrace it with a positive attitude. The night before, my mom and I enjoyed a comforting dinner and movie—my go-to remedy after another dating disappointment.

The next morning, during our group run, my good friend Alexis brightened my day with her humor and even treated me to breakfast. In the afternoon, my mom and I indulged in a relaxing pedicure, and in the evening, three of my closest friends took me out for dinner. Overall, it turned out to be a really great birthday.

Despite my doubts about Sebastian's kindness, a quality I highly valued in a partner—I couldn't deny the feelings I had for him. Haven't we all been drawn to a bad boy at some point? With encouragement from my running friend, Cara, I sent one final text: "Hello again. I promise this is the last time. Because you appreciate honesty... I was deeply disappointed and shocked by your words. I don't believe I'm completely inept in the intimacy department. I genuinely enjoyed your company, I'm very attracted to you, and I'd love to have one more date."

Days passed with no response from Sebastian. To add to my disappointment, I received an email from eHarmony saying "Be the first to meet him." It turned out Sebastian had joined eHarmony, and we were matched. I promptly closed the notification, realizing it was time to move on.

As I drove home from a new-member church gathering recommended by my friends Anna and Brian, a thunderstorm was raging outside. At the event, I learned that Denver has the highest per capita rate of alcohol-related emergency room visits in the country, making the city feel pretty isolated and desolate. Plus, with only 6 percent of Coloradans attending church, Denver is the lowest among major cities nationwide.

Sitting with these stats and my own solitude that night—just me, my books, and Jessie hiding under the bed—it felt strangely poetic and almost magical. I found myself wondering if following

God's or the Universe's guidance would bring me some comfort. Even though I'd known about this idea for a while, I realized I hadn't really embraced it until now. There was something oddly relieving about letting go of control and trusting the Universe to lead me.

On a mid-July morning, I decided to try a Reiki healing session. Reiki uses twelve hand positions to clear energy blocks in the body, aiming to promote physical, emotional, or spiritual healing. My Reiki healer was a friendly and talkative thirty-three-year-old single man with colorful tattoos covering his arms. He shared his journey into Reiki, which began with a vision of a white tiger during meditation. This vision led him to train under a Reiki teacher and leave behind a successful career in sales.

I was initially intrigued by his story, especially since it aligned with what I'd been reading. However, I left the session feeling pretty much the same as before. We talked a lot during the session, which might have interfered with the visual or insightful experiences he had mentioned. He did suggest that Reiki could positively impact my love life and promised to follow up, recognizing that I tend to process experiences slowly.

Later that week, out of the blue, Sebastian reached out via text message. He confessed, "I really like you. You have many, if not most, of the qualities I want in a partner. But that night was so awkward, I didn't know how to handle it."

Taken aback, I replied, "I'm surprised to hear from you. We didn't communicate well. What do you want—to try again, or just closure?"

"Let's meet and talk it out. We can either work things out or at least learn from the experience. I can make time today."

"Okay, but promise to keep it civil."

I was scheduled to go hiking with Tyler and told Sebastian I'd update him afterward, which I did. No response came. Hours later, I texted again, "I guess tonight isn't a good time for you after all?" Still, no reply.

Finally, feeling frustrated but unwilling to accept being ignored, I texted the next day, "Sebastian, for heaven's sake, we like each other. What happened isn't that big a deal. I don't want you making a mountain out of a molehill. If it's a deal-breaker for you, just say so. But decide."

Meanwhile, I continued dating:

Ian: A forty-something entrepreneur based in Breckenridge who thrives on rock and ice climbing. Our date at Elitch Gardens Theme and Water Park and drinks downtown showed a gap between his online persona and reality—he seemed older and less patient than expected. Nevertheless, he was a true gentleman, treating me with genuine respect. While the date was enjoyable, our different locations hinted that it might not lead to anything more.

Miles: A charismatic thirty-five-year-old businessman with a flair for the dramatic, Miles had rubbed shoulders with Hollywood stars during his time in LA. Our meeting at a wine bar sparked an immediate, genuine connection that reminded me of my carefree days in Prague. It made me question why I didn't live more fearlessly all the time—maybe it's due to judgment or a desire to always do the right thing. Talking with him made me realize how naive I was about men and the serious side of dating. According to Miles, the physical aspect of a relationship is crucial for men—they need to feel a strong physical connection early on. In contrast, women usually focus on conversation, affection, and getting to know each other's social circles. Miles and I continued to see each other sporadically due to his busy travel schedule, but things never progressed beyond that.

Will: A cute, witty thirty-five-year-old engineer who has a passion for rock climbing. We went out four times before he finally kissed me, and then he started traveling for work and we lost touch.

Nicholas: A charming thirty-three-year-old engineer and Air Force grad. Our initial dinner was sweet, and we followed it up with a motorcycle ride, a movie, and dinner at his place. But as our dates continued, it became clear he didn't have the compassion I needed, and I got tired of constantly deflecting his advances.

My new attitude became "Forget it all." Fed up with the traditional dating advice I'd followed for years, I decided to throw it out the window—maybe inspired by my recent Reiki experiences. Usually, women are told to stay in their feminine state, let men come to them, and just "receive." But I was done being passive. What if I took charge and made things happen?

On the flip side, there's Occam's razor—the simplest explanation is often the right one—which suggested maybe Sebastian just wasn't that into me. But where's life without a little risk?

So, I took a leap and called Sebastian, leaving a message. When he got back to Denver, he texted me asking what was up. I replied confidently, "I don't usually chase after guys, but I'm making an exception here. I think you might have a wrong impression of me. If you want to come over and see what it could really be like between us, you're welcome to. If not, well, I've had enough embarrassment for one summer!"

He replied, "I didn't mean to embarrass you. My delivery was poor and ill-timed and mean spirited."

I texted, "Thanks for saying that."

He continued, "Well, it's true. If anyone should be embarrassed, it's me. I appreciate your offer, but I'm not sure what to say. As a guy, I want to say heck yea. But I want to be pragmatic. Sex was so nonexistent in my marriage that I would rather stay single for the rest of my life than go through that again."

I responded, "It's your call. If sex is your main concern, I can address that. If there's something else and you just don't see it with me, I can understand that too."

Eventually, he called, and we arranged for him to come over the next day.

I was buzzing with excitement thanks to my newfound, fearless attitude. Even though we didn't talk about what had happened, there was something about being with Sebastian that felt really special—like the joy I'd had with Chris.

Sebastian stayed the night, and it felt like we had that deep, intimate connection you see in honeymooners. He planned to take me to breakfast, but a work call interrupted us. He suggested we meet up again that weekend, but he ended up getting sick. The next week, he was buried in a work emergency, which left me feeling disappointed. Thinking about his illness and stress, I texted, "Thinking of you, hope you're doing better."

His quick reply was "Working, lots." When I followed up about the room he was building, he just said, "Nearly." And that was it. I understood our casual arrangement, but I couldn't shake the disappointment, especially since he had been so enthusiastic about our plans.

I thought about taking a Steve Harvey approach, considering he might be emotionally unavailable due to work stress. But deep down, I knew if he truly cared, he would make an effort. I'd been through this before, and it became clear: he was avoiding commitment, leaving me in limbo, which was the hardest part.

Eastern philosophies talk about embracing impermanence, while Buddhism suggests sitting with your feelings, accepting them, making peace, and then letting them go. Evelyn's advice kept running through my mind: "Focus on your blessings, find the answers within, and learn the lessons."

In the end, all I could do was breathe, laugh at the absurdity of it all, and trust that clarity would come when it was ready.

Just as I was about to give up on Sebastian, he called one night and told me he'd been working brutal fourteen-hour days. He asked if I wanted to hang out on Friday, but when the day came, he was too tired to come over. Instead, he invited me to his place, but just as I was about to head out, he texted saying he wasn't feeling well and wouldn't be much fun. He had also invited me to an outdoor movie with his friends on Saturday, but I already had plans I didn't want to cancel just for him.

The weekend passed with no word from him until I texted after a motorcycle ride and dinner with another date, asking, "Hi! How are you? Will I get to see you this week?"

He replied right away with, "Do you want to?"

I said yes, but when he didn't follow up, I asked, "Are you okay?"

He said, "I didn't think you really wanted to drive to my place to see me."

I told him, "I don't care where we are, I just want to see you." He finally softened, and on Monday, I drove to his place in Broomfield with Jessie. Sebastian made dinner, and it turned into another great night of cuddling, talking, and watching *The Bachelorette*. He even offered to support me at my upcoming triathlon and was excited to help me cook dinner for my mom and aunts who were visiting from the Midwest. As he walked me to my car that night, he gave me a sweet goodnight kiss.

On Tuesday night, he called me, which felt like a step forward for us. Sebastian stayed over on Friday before my mom and I did the triathlon the next morning, which went really well. Even though Sebastian seemed a bit distant and grumpy, blaming it on the heat, I still drove him back to his car after the event, and we talked about making plans to see each other again.

We decided to go to Elitch's on Tuesday using free coupons. The day started great—Sebastian was affectionate, and we were having a lot of fun, like I used to with Chris. But I noticed he never offered to drive; I always did. He asked if I'd eaten, but throughout the night, he seemed a little checked out, which reminded me of Luca.

We decided to wait in line for the Mind Eraser roller coaster, which was supposed to

be a forty-five-minute wait, but it felt like it took longer. Sebastian started getting irritated when kids cut in line, and he spoke up, clearly frustrated, which made me uncomfortable. When more kids tried to cut later, he negotiated with them to let us go ahead, but he was still upset about the whole thing. His attitude was starting to remind me of my ex-husband, Jason.

Even after we finally rode the roller coaster, Sebastian's mood didn't get any better. He complained about the wait, criticized the park staff, and even brought down the mood of a cheerful worker—just like Jason used to do. As we left the ride, he kept venting to people about the wait, and I tried to steer him away. When I asked what he needed after a bad day, he snapped at me, telling me not to bombard him with questions.

At that moment, I realized this wasn't what I wanted. Sebastian's poor coping skills and attitude sealed the deal for me, and I let him know. That was the end of our relationship.

Years later, out of the blue, Sebastian emailed me with some surprising news. He said he was doing much better since his diagnosis.

"What diagnosis?" I asked.

"Bipolar II," he replied. "I'm on medication now. I've stopped drinking, and I've realized I do better working with hands-on work, like remodeling houses, instead of trying to run a business. I couldn't handle that stress. I'm much more grounded now."

"Good to hear," I thought, "because trying to balance that emotional roller coaster felt like building a house on quicksand."

Adam: A thirty-six-year-old engineer from my running club surprised me by asking me to dinner after one of our runs. I couldn't believe it—he knew my personality and had only ever seen me sweaty and without makeup! We met for dinner at a nice restaurant, had wine, an appetizer, entrée, and dessert. He paid, walked me to my car, and we hugged, locking eyes, but didn't kiss. He asked me out for dinner two more times and even hiking once, but still no kiss. I was wondering if he just wanted to be friends. Then one night in November, I visited his new house. We drank wine, snuggled while watching a movie, and finally kissed. But then he skipped over everything else and asked if I wanted to spend the night. The kisses were nice, but I decided to take it slow and went home. Good thing, too, because he got busy with work, dropped out of the running club for the winter, and that ended up being our last date before he met someone else.

Freddie: A thirty-five-year-old financial manager who rode a motorcycle and lived with a roommate in Boulder was another intriguing match. We met for drinks, and the following weekend, we had a picnic in a park by the lake. He brought wine, cheese, and crackers. We talked about religion and life philosophies, ending the night with a warm kiss and him telling me I was worth the drive. It was a romantic evening. Unfortunately, he left for a vacation to the Galapagos Islands for a couple of weeks and then got sick. We tried to stay in touch but never ended up seeing each other again.

Mitchell: In September, I met Mitchell, a thirty-eight-year-old, incredibly handsome fireman who had a soft spot for dogs. He had everything: sexy brown eyes, kissable lips, and a lean, muscular build. He was tall, ruggedly good looking, funny, and always polite. We spent four amazing hours at the dog park, where he told stories that had me laughing so hard my stomach hurt. When another dog started a scuffle with Jessie, Mitchell's calm presence and reassurance were exactly what I needed. We said goodbye with a hug, a kiss on the cheek, and him saying he had a blast. After that, daily texts and calls became our thing.

I found out that his last serious relationship ended a few months prior—a long-distance thing for a couple of years. He also casually mentioned how most people hate being alone, hinting at his surprise that I'd been divorced for over five years.

We had another fun four-hour happy hour together, but after that, communication seemed to fade, and I assumed he was losing interest. Still, we kept texting here and there until I decided to take a chance and invite him and his dog, Athena, over for dinner the next week. I expected him to be noncommittal or take his time replying, but to my surprise, he was excited and even sent a photo of them both, saying how pumped they were for our dinner date.

As we kept texting, he remembered my quirky term "mush" for snuggling. I joked, "Most people don't catch on to my language so fast."

He replied, "I'm not 'most,' but I guess I'll have to prove that to you."

I teased back, "That's true, you're definitely not 'most,' but you can keep proving it."

He responded, "Fair enough. And I will. I'm really looking forward to seeing you and Jessie again—and sharing some merlot."

When Mitchell and Athena showed up, he greeted me with a kiss, and we spent hours talking. Well, mostly he talked, but I loved every minute of it. He even showed me a few Krav Maga moves, and the feel of his arms around me was absolutely mesmerizing.

After our date, he sent a sweet thank-you text, saying, "I loved the company, the wine, and the kiss... :)" That led to a long phone call where he invited Jessie and me to his place for dinner, suggested we visit his aunt and uncle together, and even offered to join me for my first Krav Maga class.

It took a couple more weeks, but Mitchell finally invited Jessie and me over for dinner. His house was spotless, and he made delicious sangria, green chili burritos, and cookies for dessert. How can I even describe my attraction to him? He was incredibly good looking, respectful, surprisingly compassionate, and could cook! He talked a lot and didn't ask much about me, but his encouragement and sensitivity in the moment—like when he patiently taught me Krav Maga—had me feeling like I was in heaven. Snuggling on the couch with my hot fireman and our dogs nearby made it a perfect evening. Not long after that, he left for a weeklong trip to Ireland.

When Mitchell got back from his trip, the mixed messages started. He called me, and we ended up talking for four hours. At one point, I said, "I figured you'd be sleeping all day after getting back from Ireland."

"So, that's why I haven't heard from you," he said, hinting he wanted me to call him (which I took as a good sign). Trying to keep things balanced, I gathered the courage to ask, "Do you want to get together tomorrow night?"

"I've got to work the next day, and I like to go to bed early before a shift. I'd rather have a proper night together than just a quick meetup. Maybe Sunday?" So, we made some vague plans for Sunday (which didn't feel so promising).

Sunday came, and I didn't hear from him until midafternoon.

"I have a cold and don't feel great," he explained (definitely not a great sign). "But I wanted to make sure you knew I wasn't blowing you off," he added (a better sign). We ended up talking on the phone for another four hours (which felt positive).

Then one Friday night in early November, Mitchell texted around 8:00 p.m. and finally asked if I wanted to see the firehouse on Saturday (a good move). Of course, I said yes! It had been two weeks since we last saw each other (which wasn't as great).

I showed up at the firehouse for dinner at 5:30 p.m. Mitchell gave me a tour of where they slept, worked out, and watched sports on a big-screen TV with five huge, comfy reclining chairs lined up. Then I joined five rugged firefighters for dinner, and I have to admit, I felt a bit out of place. After dinner, we watched football, and not sure how long to stay, I decided to head out at halftime.

"I guess I should get going."

"Let me walk you to your car." We shared a goodnight kiss (which was a good sign).

"I'm glad you came. I'll text you."

We had tentative plans to get together the next day, but they fell through. I didn't push the issue since he was still feeling sick (not a great sign). I ended up back in that uncertain stage where I wasn't sure where the relationship was going, and it seemed like it wasn't heading where I hoped.

So, when a potential date from the previous summer reached out, I decided to meet him.

Weston: A thirty-five-year-old independently wealthy animal lover who had even fostered a baby zebra that went running with him. We finally met for coffee. We initially connected in June, but he'd been out of town since then and just reached out. Weston is truly one of the most amazing guys I've ever met—smart, open, vulnerable, and handsome. His life felt like something out of a Danielle Steel novel. He might have been out of my league, but he did suggest a second date. The only catch? He'd be out of town for a few weeks. Why does it always seem like the timing is off with these guys?

By late November, Mitchell's mixed messages had really shaken my confidence and sent me into a whirlwind of anxiety that I just couldn't shake. I tried everything—challenged my thoughts, ran with friends, walked Jessie with Tyler, got a massage, took a yoga class, ate healthy, watched dating videos on how women can better relate to men, and went shopping with my mom. Eventually,

I cracked open a bottle of wine, and that seemed to do the trick.

This anxiety really showed me how far I was from that peaceful state all those self-help books talk about, the kind that stays calm even in chaos. I tried to follow all the advice:

- Live in the moment.
- Appreciate the beauty in winter.
- Be kind to yourself.
- Find happiness on your own.

But when I sat still, the deep, lonely ache in my heart—that only a romantic relationship could fill—just wouldn't let up.

Spiritual advice seemed to suggest that if you can't be happy on your own, you're out of luck. As my friend Melissa would say, "Oh, for fuck's sake."

I'd been managing on my own for thirty-seven years, so logically, I should be okay if things didn't work out with Mitchell. But I didn't want to face the truth: he might just not be that into me. It was another disappointment, another reality check that I might end up alone. This attitude wasn't helping. Sometimes I got caught up in it, but other times I knew I deserved a good man. Dating can be a tough cycle. How does anyone rise above it without a little help?

Evelyn said, "People like us—mental health professionals, engineers, lawyers—we're too much in our heads and not enough in our hearts. Sit with your feelings, journal about them, and then be grateful."

Back to Mitchell. He kept reaching out with texts and calls, and after a little nudging, he finally invited me out for dinner on a chilly Monday night in December. When I arrived, Mitchell looked really sharp in a button-up shirt and a sweater as he stood to greet me. To calm my nerves and seem more confident, I had a glass of wine—not the best move, but we had a good time. I'd read in Christian Carter's e-book that "challenging" a guy can spark attraction, so I asked him, "What are you looking for that you haven't found yet?" I don't remember his exact answer, if he even gave one, but the conversation quickly shifted back to his ex. She had trouble communicating; she didn't get his perspective, and his dad wasn't a fan. He always flew to see her, and she rarely visited him. He said something about things working out as they should, sounding like he was trying to convince himself of that.

After that, the texts and calls started to drop off. We stopped talking daily, and he started initiating less often.

According to Evelyn and relationship experts, I should work on my communication and take some risks with vulnerability. I wondered if it was too late for that with Mitchell. Even if it was, I wanted to face my fears and practice with him. It seems so basic; the "I" message I teach my students: "I feel ___ because ___. I'd like it if ___." No blame, letting the other person choose, and being willing to walk away if needed. Back to setting boundaries.

I gave him a call, and we had a pretty good chat with some laughs, which was nice. I tried to be casual and said, "I know we talked about getting together this week, but I wanted to check if anything's changed and if you still want to?" I'd read that asking, "Has something changed?" can lead to the truth. Without missing a beat, he said he did want to get together. We discussed which night would work best, and Saturday seemed good, even though he was working the next day. So we made "tentative plans" for Saturday and said we'd figure something else out if that didn't work. Not sure if I cleared much up, but okay.

Some philosophies suggest giving space in these situations to let the truth come out. By Saturday, the day of our "tentative" plans, I hadn't heard a peep from him since our last chat almost a week ago. We never ended up meeting again. His silence was my answer. Are you kidding me?

My good friend Tyler said there are different types of dates: the one where you know right away there's no connection, the ones you go on a few times, the ones you date for several months, the ones that last six months to a year, and then the ones you marry. He said it was actually a good thing that Mitchell and I dated as long as we did. It meant he liked me a lot but just wasn't falling in love. I guess Tyler's take is a bit more positive.

I watched *He's Just Not That Into You*, and it has the same message as all the advice I've come across: when you stop trying so hard, let go, and focus on yourself, that's when things start happening. If things end and you're alone, it's really making space for something better. But are these books and movies actually based on real-life experiences, or are they there just to offer false hope and make money? What if you've done everything they say—made space for something better—and that better thing never comes? Aren't these supposed to be "universal laws"? Maybe there are no universal laws, just ideal ones. It comes down to a choice: live in disappointment or not? Keep your faith or not?

In a last-ditch effort, I went with my newly single friend to a speed-dating event. She didn't find anyone, but I met Mark and Elliot, which led to me having dated a total of twenty men since all this started.

Mark: We met at an old-fashioned burger joint using a Groupon he had. During the date, I found out he was only twenty-five. We were at opposite ends of the age spectrum for the speed-dating event that night. I was too shy to tell him I was twelve years older, so even though he was a nice guy, I let that fizzle out pretty quickly.

Elliot: Elliot, a thirty-four-year-old real estate guy, was into meditation and energy. He took me out to dinner and said he liked my "energy," calling it a small bright light. He claimed his energy was bigger, more powerful, and unique. He said people either were drawn to him or avoided him because he reflected their unfinished business (hello, red flag?). Despite that, he was interesting to talk to, so I decided to give him a shot.

He wanted to join me and my friends for New Year's, which seemed a bit odd for a second date. Elliot was on a strict eating and fitness regimen to gain muscle. Instead of enjoying the appetizers Alexis made, he had his own peanut butter and jelly sandwich on Ezekiel bread—basically gluten-free and not very tasty. Some might see this as overly rigid, while others might think it shows he's confident and not swayed by others. He also didn't drink, and I spent the night wondering if he was having a good time. He was a good sport about it but left shortly after midnight, since he was strict about his sleep schedule too.

We made plans to get together the following Saturday night. We talked and texted occasionally throughout the week, but I was busy with work and didn't always respond to his texts promptly. So, I got a text message on Friday: "Forget our Saturday plans."

"I'm confused. What's going on?"

"If you're not going to text back right away, clearly you're not interested."

"I'm not always right by my phone. I was looking forward to seeing you though."

"Oh, okay. We can still plan it then."

For Saturday, it was my turn to drive an hour south to meet him, since he had driven to Denver twice to meet me. He wanted to make dinner at his house and watch a movie. However, it started snowing, and I had been battling migraines recently. I called him and said, "It's snowing here already. What do you think about rescheduling? I'm hesitant to drive an hour each way in the snow, and I'm not ready to spend the night."

"What? We made plans. It's your turn to drive here. You're just a flake like all the other women."

"Okay, well, it has been nice getting to know you, but I don't think this is going to work out. I wish you the best though."

"What? You're breaking up with me?"

"Well, you're a great person; we're just not the right fit."

"You're the one being flaky! I was making time for you. I have other things I could be doing and other women I could be dating…"

"Okay, well, I've got to go now. Goodbye."

"Now you're hanging up on—"

Click.

Over the past year, as I perhaps overly focused on dating, I've come across tons of advice from friends, dating experts, articles, and even Evelyn. Here's a quick rundown of the current wisdom that's supposed to lead to happily ever after.

Dos:

1. **Be happy and independent.** Enjoy your own interests.
2. **Smile.** It's inviting and warm.
3. **Make eye contact.** Really look into their eyes.
4. **Stay positive.** Keep things light and humorous; ask lots of questions about him; offer to pay on first dates.
5. **Date multiple people.** Keep your options open.
6. **Mirror his interest.** Match his enthusiasm, but don't overdo it.
7. **Trust your intuition.** It usually knows best.
8. **Stir emotions.** Share your opinions.
9. Don't tolerate bad behavior; don't seem needy.
10. **Embrace feminine energy.** Own your emotions, show your quirks, cook if you like, but let him handle things like opening a jar of pickles.

11. **Express appreciation.** Make him feel respected and valued.
12. **Inspire growth.** Encourage him to chase his dreams.
13. **Love and accept him.** Appreciate him for who he is.
14. **Give space.** If he pulls away, let him.
15. **Use feeling language.** Address issues with "I feel" statements.
16. **Empower him.** Praise the behaviors you like instead of complaining about the ones you don't.

Don'ts:

1. **Don't be too independent.** Show that you need him.
2. **Don't blend in.** Stand out and be memorable.
3. **Don't be too eager.** Keep a balanced approach.
4. **Don't play the victim.** Avoid generalizing all men as jerks.
5. **Don't hook up on the first date.** Take it slow.
6. **Don't contact him first.** Let him reach out after the first date.
7. **Don't respond too quickly.** Give it some time.
8. **Don't make too many demands.** Be considerate of his time and emotions, especially early on.
9. **Don't dwell on why.** If it doesn't work out, just move on.
10. **Don't nag.** Avoid repetitive requests.
11. **Don't assume exclusivity.** Have an open conversation about it.
12. **Don't bring up exclusivity first.** Or say "I love you" first.

Watch Out For:
- **Men who can't be alone.** They may smother you.
- **Men over forty.** Especially those who've never married or have short relationship histories; they might have an avoidant attachment style.
- **Recently separated or divorced men.** They could be on the rebound.
- **Significantly older or younger men.** Different priorities or lifestyle differences could complicate things.

Navigating the dating scene can feel like a whirlwind of advice and rules, and it's easy to get overwhelmed. But at the core of it all, dating is about connecting, discovering, and growing.

As you sift through all the tips, remember that the most important thing is to stay true to yourself. Embrace what makes you unique and let your genuine self shine. The journey might have its ups and downs, but each step helps you get closer to what you really want and need in a partner.

Coco Chanel once said, "Just be the best self you can possibly be and remember that a girl should be two things: who and what she wants." So be brave, stay positive, and trust that, with each step, you're getting closer to finding the right match. Keep your heart open, and remember, the right person will appreciate you for who you are.

Unexpected Gifts from the Revolving Door

The gifts from dating—where do I start? First and foremost, dating helps clarify what you truly want in a partner. Even though I'm still mastering healthy boundaries, dating has given me a chance to get better at it and avoid wasting time in the wrong relationships. For example, moving on from Sebastian was tough, but it made me realize that kindness and compassion are nonnegotiable for me. Dating also teaches you how to be emotionally flexible and resilient. Dealing with mixed signals and uncertainty, like with Mitchell, has helped me appreciate my own worth and be okay with the fact that sometimes things just don't work out. Overall, here are a few lessons my twenty dates taught me about seeing things clearly:

- **Embrace Positive Self-Talk:** Just because things don't work out with one person (or even twenty) doesn't mean you're unworthy of love or that there's something wrong with you. Dating is full of complexities that rarely have anything to do with you personally.
- **Pay Attention to Your Body Language:** Sit up straight, make eye contact, and smile. Not only does it make you appear more confident, but it can also boost your own self-assurance.
- **Don't Believe Everything He Says Early On**: In the early stages (from the first few dates to the first few months), don't get too caught up on what he says (e.g., "You're so cute and funny!" "I really like you." "I can't wait to see you again." "You mean the world to me." "I haven't felt like

this in a long time."). Men might mean these things in the moment, but only for that moment. They might not stick around, and that's why it's important to take things slow and let them earn our trust.

- **Watch His Actions, Not His Words:** If he's not initiating phone calls or texts, he's not "the one," at least not right now. Even if he says nice things and responds positively to your texts, he might just be being polite because he's too afraid to tell you how he really feels.
- **Stay Graceful Even When Hurt:** Sometimes being graceful, even when you're hurt, can make him reconsider and come back. And if not, at least you can feel good about yourself, and he knows he didn't break you (even if he did).
- **Don't Be Too Picky, but Don't Settle:** Give a guy up to three dates to see if there's a connection. After that, think about whether you feel good, energized, or happy around him. Many good men are diamonds in the rough, but if you're still not feeling, move on. Settling isn't worth it, because it just wastes time and leads to dissatisfaction, which can cause all sort of problems, from affairs to health issues.
- **Take Breaks When Needed:** It's important to step back and recharge when things get overwhelming, but don't let it deter you from continuing your journey.

Conclusion

When we are no longer able to change a situation, we are challenged to change ourselves.

—Victor Frankl

There comes a point when you have to choose between living in disappointment and loneliness or embracing happiness and contentment. For me, that moment hit in January. I was drained from dating—commuting to the city, finding new spots to meet, and keeping conversations going. The ups and downs, guessing games, and constant rejections were wearing me out. I was fed up with giving more than I got, both in dating and in my relationships. It became clear that chasing a relationship or starting a family wasn't the key to my happiness.

Around this time, I heard someone talk about "living in the moment" with such enthusiasm. I'd heard of it before but never really got it, even after a year of meditation. But my mind was finally worn out, and I didn't want to think anymore. I stopped dating and, for the first time, felt genuinely uninterested in putting energy into it. I wasn't scared like I used to be. I finally experienced the contentment that all the self-help books rave about. The past and future had become too painful because of all the disappointments, so the present started to feel like a relief.

I felt a new sense of freedom and lightness in my heart. I found true joy in spending time with my students at work, Jessie at home, my happily paired-up friends, and just living without the weight of disappointment or longing. But old patterns can creek back in easily, and I still had lapses and recurring thoughts.

With all the books, experts, and philosophies making the path to happiness sound so straightforward, I wondered if some people just find it naturally or if it only comes when you're truly ready. Maybe you can't force it before its time. I followed all the advice, tried to let go of judgment, and still felt stuck.

Then came that moment of realization. I'd surrendered to my losses, and happiness was my only choice. Even then, it wasn't an instant transformation. It's a process that takes effort and doesn't always fit the "do this, get that" formula that experts suggest. It's not about getting a reward in the end; it's about making the present more manageable and easing the intensity of frustration, guilt, sadness, or fear.

In *Life 101*, John-Roger and Peter McWilliams emphasize that achieving happiness requires significant strength and effort. They argue that happiness isn't easy, and demands qualities like courage, persistence, and resilience. While thinking happy thoughts seems simple, maintaining them amid life's pressures and challenges takes real strength, practice, patience, and discipline.

Taoism shares this view. In Diane Dreher's *The Tao of Inner Peace*, there's a chapter titled "Creating Greater Joy in Life" that talks about finding joy through purpose, detachment, order, adventure, and humor. Many major philosophies agree on this. The book points out that too often, people look for happiness outside themselves (like I did in my search for love), which leads to constant strain and dissatisfaction. Taoism advises us to look within and follow our own rhythms instead.

The book on Taoism explains that a joyful life is both flexible and well-structured. Peace of mind doesn't come easily; it takes discipline. Taoist discipline involves appreciating the everyday, moving in sync with life, maintaining good posture, listening carefully, speaking truthfully, and staying present. Harmony requires effort, and it's easy to slip into negative thought patterns like anger and self-pity.

The book also points out that we often take life too seriously. Laughter helps us remember that everything is temporary and that life flows through changes. We can either embrace these changes or resist them, but resisting only causes pain. Plus, laughter boosts endorphins, improves breathing, strengthens the immune system, relaxes muscles, and reduces stress.

After starting to grasp these concepts and no longer feeling a constant longing for something outside myself, life threw me another curveball. My beloved dog Jessie, who had been with me for nearly twelve years, passed away peacefully at home in May from liver disease.

I'd known this moment was coming, but I never knew how I'd handle it. Losing Jessie was losing my best friend, my family, my rock through all the other tough times.

I took it day by day, breathing through the grief. My dear friends rallied around me, and I found comfort in the poem "Rainbow Bridge." Eventually, I managed to clean my house and move forward.

Then I met Robert, a thirty-eight-year-old Bostonian with a rugged charm. His dog passed away two days before Jessie. We crossed paths at a pet loss support group, and I was moved by the tears he shed while sharing memories of his dog. Afterward, we went for a drink, and I found myself genuinely captivated by him.

That evening, Robert planned a weekend date for us—a trip to the art museum followed by happy hour downtown. He even joined me and my friends at a Rockies game, charming us all. We spent relaxed evenings at my place, enjoying appetizers and drinks under the stars. When I got my new puppy, Gracie, he was there to support me, and he cheered me on at my tennis matches. It felt like the start of something special.

But reality set in. Robert gently admitted he didn't feel the same spark, so I accepted his decision, focused on myself, and we stayed friends.

Later that summer, I went to my high school reunion feeling a bit out of place. Despite being voted "most spirited" as a cheerleader two decades earlier, I showed up alone with a mix of anticipation and uncertainty. Standing with some acquaintances, I noticed Jason (not my ex-husband Jason). As he talked about his kids and life in Arizona, his warmth and charm stood out. Our conversation revealed his thoughtful side and his doubts about his current relationship, which he described as a rebound after his divorce. In a candid moment, I shared my own desire for a deep connection. The night turned out to be unexpectedly fun, and I agreed to join friends for the second part of the reunion the next evening. As I was leaving, Jason's comment, "Leaving already?" stuck with me, though I didn't think too much of it at the time.

The next night kicked off with lots of laughs with my old girlfriends. After dinner, Jason joined us and bought me a glass of wine. We spent the rest of the evening playing poker, in line with the "Casino night" theme. My friends started teasing me, saying, "I think he likes you. He's been leaning into you all night." Later on, Jason invited me to join everyone at a restaurant, and as we were chatting, he leaned in, and we shared a sweet kiss that sent a thrilling rush of excitement through me.

True to our high school selves, we partied late into the night, ending up on the floor of someone's parents' house. In a candid moment, Jason confessed, "I stalked you on Facebook to see if you were single."

My playful response was "Are we friends on Facebook?"

"I'm so glad to see you here tonight. I was disappointed when you left early last night," Jason admitted.

"I'm glad I came too."

Later that night, he shared, "I definitely feel a spark with you, but I felt shy admitting it in case the feelings aren't returned."

"There are sparks for me too."

"This feels so comfortable with you."

And he was right; it did feel comfortable together. Could it be true? A guy who had moved me in just a few hours was captivated by me too?

The next morning, Jason dropped me off at my car, looking adorable in a backward baseball cap. He promised to text and call, and we kissed goodbye. As I drove away, I couldn't help but think, "God has a sense of humor—same name as my ex-husband and long distance like my ex-fiancé."

He began texting me that day and set up times to call. Jason ended things with his girlfriend that week and kept consistent contact with me. He shared, "I feel much better now. It had been bothering me for a while. I'm really into someone else..." He quickly planned visits to Denver and even suggested a weekend getaway in Santa Fe, New Mexico. I felt at ease with him, and everything seemed to fall into place. Even though I was hesitant about another long-distance relationship, this one felt different, and I found myself truly open to it, especially after Jason returned to Denver for a visit.

On a Thursday evening, Jason showed up at my door looking even more handsome than I remembered. We hugged right away, and as we enjoyed the dinner I had prepared, everything felt effortless. He stayed with his parents that night out of respect, but the next evening, he surprised me with flowers and a toy for Gracie. We had pizza and then a cozy night at home. Being with him felt magical, and the attraction between us was undeniable.

Saturday was pure joy as we savored doing nothing together. Later, he treated me to a lovely dinner where I mentioned concerns about the financial aspect of a long-distance relationship. Jason reassured me, saying, "I like you enough to give it a try."

Sunday came too soon, and we watched a Broncos game before a tender goodbye Monday morning at the airport. That week, he offered to buy my plane ticket to Arizona for a visit during my fall break in October. He planned to visit Denver in November, and he invited me to spend Christmas with his family.

We stayed in touch daily, and my family and friends felt optimistic about us. It seemed like the perfect ending to this story.

But no. Ten days before my scheduled flight to Arizona, Jason called and explained, "My ex-wife needs to go to California on a business trip during the week you're supposed to be here. The kids will be with me, and it would be awkward for all of us. I'm not ready for that yet either. I've tried to think of solutions, but there aren't any."

"Is there another weekend I could come out?"

"No, not until the end of November anyway. The boys have sports every weekend, and I promised I'd be there. Right or wrong, they're my focus now. Long distance is harder than I thought. I understand if you want to break up, or we could continue casually and see each other when we can."

"I need some time to think about this."

"I understand. I'll text you later."

Days passed without hearing from him. Shocked and hurt, I realized I wasn't enough of a priority for this relationship to work. I didn't have the time, money, or energy for another man to play with my heart. So, I sent him an email, expressing my desire to either fully commit to us continuing as planned or to end things. Still, I didn't hear from him for a few more days, and as I suspected, he chose to end it. He apologized, saying it wasn't logical, and his heart couldn't commit. Later, I learned it was because he had met someone else.

The consensus was clear: I have had terrible luck with men. If you're reading this book to decide whether or not to leave your current relationship, please don't panic and think, "I can't go through all that!" Many people don't face the same challenges I've encountered. Even Evelyn didn't have any answers left. She said a prayer with me, and let me tell you, prayers do work, especially when done by an experienced pray-er like Evelyn. In *Prayer Is Good Medicine* by Larry Dossey, MD, scientific evidence shows that prayers can be effective. The book details the evidence for prayer, the controversy around it, and explains what prayer is and how to pray. More than 130 controlled laboratory studies show that prayer or a prayer-like state of compassion, empathy, and love can bring about positive changes in many types of living things, from humans to bacteria.

Although science confirms the efficacy of prayer, it cannot explain how or why, much like quantum physics. Experiments suggest that love is one of the most important factors influencing its effectiveness. Furthermore, there have been countless instances in which distant prayer succeeds without the knowledge of the recipient.

Yet, often we pray, and it doesn't seem to make a difference. That's because the answer isn't always "yes." In the failure to receive what we request, we often receive a greater gift. Consider the "Prayer of an Unknown Confederate Soldier," an often-shared but anonymous work with uncertain origins. This heartfelt prayer has circulated widely and can be found in different versions online, as well as in various historical and religious texts:

> I asked God for strength that I might achieve; I was made weak that I might learn to obey. I asked for health that I might do great things; I was given infirmity, that I might do better things. I asked for riches that I might be happy; I was given poverty that I might be wise. I asked for power that I might have the praise of men; I was given weakness that I might feel the need of God. I asked for all things that I might enjoy life; I was given life that I might enjoy all things. I got nothing that I had asked for, but everything that I had hoped for.

Looking back, I realize how fear held me back: afraid to leave my ex-husband and face life alone, afraid to move to be with Chris, afraid to let go of Paul, thinking he was my last chance at love. I was afraid to trust myself, to communicate honestly, and to disappoint others or hear uncomfortable truths.

I wish I hadn't rushed into relationships to heal a broken heart. Instead, I wish I had faced my fears, embraced solitude, and found peace within, rather than clinging to unhealthy situations. But, like grief, unlearning old patterns and adopting new ones takes time. We have to go through our own trial and error, or seek guidance, to develop healthier habits. No one can do it for us—it requires hard work, patience, and courage. Even though I resisted the healing process, everything turned out okay, and I learned so much along the way.

Recognizing patterns in relationships and within ourselves can be tricky because we often fall into them without even realizing it. Our behavior is shaped by so many things—our upbringing, worldview, and fears, just to name a few. Along the way, we pick up unhelpful thoughts and beliefs that lead to doubts about whether we're good enough, lovable, or destined to be abandoned. When we carry unhealed wounds, we tend to gravitate toward the same types of people—those who are critical, unavailable, or even abusive—hoping we can somehow rewrite the ending. We think, "Maybe this time it'll be different," believing they'll change and finally love us.

To avoid looking inward, we do all sorts of things: get into the wrong relationships, blame others, enable unhealthy behaviors, take risks, and hold on to familiar dysfunction. It's a way to dodge the painful truth, which can feel too overwhelming to face at first. But if we want to create a better life, we have to confront it. The truth is, life can be unbearable sometimes, but not always. Our wounds run deep, and it often feels harder to dig in, fix them, and heal than to stay stuck.

In *How Did I Get Here?* Barbara DeAngelis compares being stuck in a bad situation to falling asleep on a cactus. When you wake up and realize where you are, you hesitate to move because you know it'll hurt. So you stay there, stuck. But eventually, you decide it's time to get out, even though freeing yourself will be painful. Once you break free from harmful thoughts, behaviors, and patterns, you can finally heal and move forward to something better. It's tough, but it's worth it—and it might even turn out better than you expected. At that point, you can ask yourself, "What am I free to do now?" Maybe it's taking that dream trip, starting a business, picking up an old passion, or just relaxing. Whatever it is, the choice is yours.

Even if we don't always understand why things happen, the choices we make are never wasted. Somehow, they turn into something beautiful.

Epilogue

On a warm summer day, my phone buzzed with a new text message.

"Hey Sara."

It was Sebastian. He had been reaching out periodically since last winter.

"Hi. How are things?"

"Meh. How are you? How's the new guy working out?"

"Didn't work out, he ghosted me, but I'm good. On summer break now, so that's nice."

"Dinner tomorrow night? Just as friends."

"Okay. I have a meeting downtown tomorrow. How about 6:30?"

And just like that, Sebastian was back in my life. But this time, the dynamic had shifted. He was the one trying to win me over. I was hesitant, given our history, and honestly, I was enjoying some "me time" and doing my own thing. But I was also a little bored, and when he said, "Forget that summer. I was in a bad place. I've grown up a lot since then. Give me a chance to prove it," I figured, why not?

Meanwhile, I had reluctantly gone on one last Match.com date—only because I had promised I would. His name was Jack. He was nearly six feet tall, not much older than me, and had this subtle New Jersey accent that gave away his roots. That night, I went through the motions of a first date, just waiting for it to end so I could get back to my routine: spending time with my dogs, enjoying my usual sleep schedule, cooking, doing yoga, and catching up with friends. At first, nothing about Jack really stood out. He seemed like a regular guy. But, like me, his dogs were his kids, and he made me laugh, so I decided to see him again.

Sebastian and I went to a music festival, while Jack and I had a fun day at the dog park. Sebastian later came over for dinner, declaring it our best date yet. With Jack, we hit up the Santa Fe art walk, where we hilariously missed when we went in for our first kiss. Then, Sebastian went off to the mountains and didn't reach out for an entire week. Meanwhile, Jack was there to help me take one of my foster dogs to the vet early one morning before work.

Eventually, Sebastian apologized for disappearing, saying he thought giving me control of the relationship would make me more comfortable. I thanked him, gave him the Goodbye Sandwich, and kept seeing Jack.

Jack was a successful small business owner and a lacrosse player in his spare time. He had this easygoing confidence and could find humor in almost any situation. His smile was contagious, and you couldn't help but laugh along with him. Like the time he took me to a Korean BBQ spot for dinner. We had no idea what we were getting ourselves into and cringed as we watched the baby octopus curl up on the grill right in front of us. Neither of us ate much that night, but Jack jokingly suggested I bring the leftovers to work and pretend I was excited to eat them, just to freak out my coworkers. That was Jack—always finding a way to lighten the mood.

A few weeks later, Sebastian came back around, saying he wanted to date me exclusively and didn't want me seeing anyone else. I wasn't on board though—trust takes time to rebuild, and besides, I still wanted to date Jack. Surprisingly, Sebastian was okay with this, as long as he could still see me too.

Sebastian and I had one last meeting before he suddenly moved to Estes Park. He wanted to keep dating and thought a long-distance relationship might suit me since I'm so independent. He suggested I visit him in the mountains where we could hike with Gracie—he'd cook for us and spoil me rotten. He promised to drive down to see me whenever I wanted. The idea might have been appealing...but Jack. He was taking it slow, building trust, making me laugh, and not stressing me out. After all this time, when I genuinely wanted to enjoy being single, I found myself with two men interested in me. It seemed like everyone was right—you need to be happy on your own first, even if I still don't like that phrase.

One fall weekend in a cozy log cabin in the mountains, we were snuggled up next to a roaring fire, enjoying some wine. He kissed me sweetly until the dogs came bounding in, landing on top of us, happily wagging their tails and licking our faces. When our laughter settled down, he asked, "Can I call you my girlfriend now?"

I replied, "Yes, Jack. I'd love to be your girlfriend."

Three years later, we were married.

Healthy attracts healthy.

If you're curious about how things unfolded for me, let me fill you in. From the start, dating Jack felt effortless—I never worried about when I'd hear from him or whether I should reach out. Everything flowed naturally. He struck the perfect balance between giving me the security I needed and the space I craved.

Our first trip together was a weekend getaway to the mountains with the dogs. After a long, stressful work week, I was wiped out, but as soon as Gracie and I met Jack at his house and climbed into his truck, I felt instantly at ease. Even in those early days, being with him was soothing.

And despite the lack of a whirlwind chase that often stirs up butterflies and complicates relationships, I never felt like I was settling. I was genuinely happy. Meeting his friends and introducing him to mine felt completely natural. Our relationship moved at a comfortable pace—not too fast, not too slow (mostly, anyway).

For our first Christmas together, Jack surprised me with an iPad. When I excitedly told my dad Jack had bought me an expensive present, he held his breath and asked, "A ring?" We both laughed with relief when I said, "No, just an iPad."

Of course, things haven't been perfect. There have been moments when one or both of us had doubts. For example, Jack was forty when we'd been dating for almost a year, and I was falling for him, waiting for him to say "I love you" first. One night, while watching TV—probably a Lifetime movie I had chosen—Jack casually mentioned that he'd never really been in love before.

I was taken aback and asked, "Really? Never?" hoping he'd say he'd never been in love...until now. But he didn't. I even asked again, and he just said, "Yeah."

I started to panic a bit. Dating experts often say men over forty who haven't had serious relationships can be a red flag. I'm not usually a crier, but I felt my eyes welling up and got flustered. He had no idea what was going on, so I told him.

It wasn't how I imagined it, but I said, "I thought maybe you'd say you love me." I think I also explained the whole "man over forty" thing to him too.

He paused, gently hugged me, looked me in the eyes, and told me he did love me—and that his love would only grow stronger with time.

Another reason I see this relationship as healthy is a fun little thing we started early on. I told Jack that for a relationship to thrive, there should be nine positives for every one negative. It became our inside joke whenever things started to get tense. If he does something I'm not thrilled about, I'll jokingly say he owes me nine positives, and he does the same when I make a mistake. It usually makes us both smile and helps us let our guard down.

Another sign that this relationship is healthy—at least for me—is how Jack embraces my passion for our dogs. My good friend Ed once mentioned that most men might struggle with the attention I give to my dogs because they want to feel like they're the top priority. But Jack has never asked me to change how I love them, and having that part of me accepted means the world to me. Speaking of Ed, Jack is completely fine with me having the occasional lunch with him to catch up and with me going for dog walks with Tyler. Jack's trust and confidence in our relationship are incredibly reassuring. I'm confident that if he ever had any concerns, he would bring them up openly and they would be fair and reasonable.

There's so much more I could share, but that's a story for another time. For now, I'll just say this: I took my time publishing this book because it's such a personal story, but Jack and I are still going strong eleven years later. I hope this book has brought you some entertainment, comfort, and hope. My wish for you is that you discover your own version of "healthy," whatever that may look like for you.

References

Cloud, Henry, and John Townsend. *Boundaries*. Grand Rapids, MI: Zondervan, 1992.

Das, Lama Surya. *Awakening the Buddhist Heart: Cultivating Love and Spiritual Intelligence in Your Life*. New York: Broadway Books, 2000.

DeAngelis, Barbara. *How Did I Get Here? Finding Your Way to Renewed Hope and Happiness When Life and Love Take Unexpected Turns.* New York: St. Martin's Press, 2005.

Djukic, Phoenix, and Cornelia Schwarz. *Soul Vision: Living an Inspired Life.* Santa Barbara, CA: Elysium, 2009.

Dossey, Larry. *Prayer Is Good Medicine: How to Reap the Healing Benefits of Prayer.* New York: Harper Collins, 1996.

Dreher, Diane. *The Tao of Inner Peace*. New York: Penguin Group, 2000.

Engel, Beverly. *The Nice Girl Syndrome: Stop Being Manipulated and Abused and Start Standing Up for Yourself.* Hoboken, New Jersey: Wiley, 2008.

Fay, Mary Jo. *When Your "Perfect Partner" Goes Perfectly Wrong: Loving or Leaving the Narcissist in Your Life.* Parker, CO: Out of the Boxx, 2008.

Gilbert, Elizabeth. *Eat, Pray, Love.* New York: Penguin Group, 2006.

Gottman, John. *The Seven Principles for Making Marriage Work.* New York: Three Rivers Press, 1999.

Hagen, Steve. *Buddhism Plain and Simple: The Practice of Being Aware Right Now, Everyday.* New York: Broadway Books, 1997.

Harvey, Steve. *Act like a Lady, Think like a Man: What Men Really Think about Love, Relationships, Intimacy, and Commitment.* New York: Harper Collins, 2009.

Hay, Louise L. *You Can Heal Your Life.* Carlsbad, CA: Hay House, 1999.

Kasl, Charlotte. *If the Buddha Dated: A Handbook for Finding Love on a Spiritual Path.* New York: Penguin Group, 1999.

Lowndes, Leil. *How to Talk to Anyone: Master Small Talk, Improve Your Social Skills, and Build Meaningful Relationships.* New York: McGraw Hill, 2003.

Merrell, Kenneth W. *Helping Students Overcome Depression and Anxiety.* 2nd ed. New York: The Guilford Press, 2001.

Trafford, Abigail. *Crazy Time: Surviving Divorce and Building a New Life.* 3rd ed. New York: Harper Collins, 1992.

Virtue, Doreen. *Divine Guidance: How to Have a Dialogue with God and Your Guardian Angels.* New York: St. Martin's Griffin, 1998.

Wikipedia. "Attachment Theory." Last modified July 27, 2024. http://en.wikipedia.org/wiki/Attachment_theory.

About the Author

SARA HATHOR, originally from Muncie, Indiana, spent most of her life in Denver, Colorado. She holds a BS from Colorado State University, a Master of Science in Counseling and Development from Purdue University, and an Education Specialist degree in School Psychology from the University of Colorado at Denver. Sara undertook journaling as a therapeutic medium, navigating through relationship challenges and personal growth. She's the author of *Unexpected Gifts*, a testament to her journey. Today, Sara lives with her husband and two dogs, and maintains a close relationship with her supportive parents. Her story resonates with women seeking to understand and grow from their experiences.

Milton Keynes UK
Ingram Content Group UK Ltd.
UKHW041528081124
450708UK00033B/496